Library Programs for Children

To Don

Library Programs for Children

by

Taffy Jones

McFarland & Company, Inc., Publishers
Jefferson, North Carolina, and London

Photographs by Taffy Jones

British Cataloguing-in-Publication data available.

Library of Congress Cataloguing-in-Publication Data

Jones, Taffy, 1922-
   Library programs for children.

   Bibliography: p. 269.
   Includes index.
   1. Libraries, Children's—Activity programs.
2. School libraries—Activity programs. 3. Children—
Books and reading. I. Title.
Z718.1.J65 1989   027.8′222   89-42726
ISBN 0-89950-431-0 (sewn softcover; 50# alk. paper)

Manufactured in the United States of America.

McFarland & Company, Inc., Publishers
  Box 611, Jefferson, North Carolina 28640

Foreword

Librarians are busy people. If your library is small with a budget to match, you can be overwhelmed when it comes to planning and running special programs for children. They must be of a length to keep the children's attention, catchy enough to bring them back again, and it's always nice to have something to take home to show what they've learned that day. Plays, puppet shows and songs are an added bonus when performed for family and friends. But who has time to do all of these things and still keep the library running smoothly? That is the purpose of this book.

Comprehensive schedules and checklists at the beginning of each chapter assist you with the planning and execution of each program. The author has tried to keep craft projects simple and uses inexpensive materials with ready-made patterns for your convenience. There are easy-to-perform plays and songs meant to be enjoyed by all. A bibliography at the end of each chapter saves time when looking for books to display during your program.

You'll find this book useful and fun when it's time for your next children's program at the library!

Betty Gunrud
Tuftonboro Center School
Center Tuftonboro, New Hampshire

Contents

Contents

Special Thanks...

To Anne Swartz, children's librarian at the Fort Pierce Public Library, Fort Pierce, Florida, and Betty Gunrud, librarian at the Tuftonboro Central School, Center Tuftonboro, New Hampshire, for their encouragement and help in this project.

To the artists, who added greatly to the book: Lomie Helmich, Bette Allen, Carol Pfenning, Dianne Taylor Hochreiter, Lenora Hawkins, and Brian Taft Jones; and to Patrick J. Peters for the poetry.

To Ronald S. Jones, Ph.D., children's psychologist, Plymouth-Canton Schools, Plymouth, Michigan; John M. Harmes, M.A., children's psychologist, Newburyport Schools, Newburyport, Mass.; and Everett M. Woodman, D. Ed., now of Kliatt Paper Back Books for Young Readers, Newton, Mass., and former president of Colby College, New London, New Hampshire; for their guidance.

To Eunice Pomaville for manuscript typing.

And to the many library people who kept me on the path and inspired me to write this book for their use:

Tammy Boggus, children's librarian at the Palm Bay Public Library, Palm Bay, Florida

Lynne Butler, children's librarian at the Meadow Lane Public Library, West Melbourne, Florida

Rosemary Dyke, children's librarian at the Melbourne Public Library, Melbourne, Florida

Julie Sturgeon, assistant children's librarian at the Melbourne Public Library, Melbourne, Florida

Judy Mueller, LWP of the new Lakewood Park Public Library, Fort Pierce, Florida

Betty Wilkens, character in the book, former children's librarian at the Stuart Public Library and now librarian at St. Joseph's Elementary School, Stuart, Florida

Special Thanks

Victoria S. Johnson, "Book Witch" puppetry at the Stuart Public Library, Stuart, Florida

Carol Trink, director of the Fort Pierce Community Center, Fort Pierce, Florida

John Perkins, librarian at the Tuftonboro Free Library, Center Tuftonboro, New Hampshire

Louise Gehman, librarian at the Wolfeboro Public Library, Wolfeboro, New Hampshire

Ruby Pearson, librarian at the Ossipee Public Library, Ossipee, New Hampshire

Adele Taylor, Moultonboro Public Library

Introduction

Library Programs for Children is a book designed to bring children to the library, to make the busy librarian's workload lighter, and to show children that books can be special friends.

The book consists of ten library programs for children in grades 1–4 and ten for preschoolers and kindergarten students. The programs are grouped around five themes: Bears, Mice, Dinosaurs, Indians, and Bookworms. Each theme offers a long and a short program for each of the two age groups. Every program has its own coordinating activities, which include story time, library time (for learning about the library), games, crafts, music, drama, and snack time. For every theme there is an original play for the children to perform.

The schedules are not intended to be rigid with regard to time or activities. You may want to expand or cut, or substitute one activity for another. Two activities I particularly recommend for use in any of the programs are "Sleuthing Out the Card Catalog" (page 43) and "The Card Catalog Game" (page 206). These basic introductions to an important library skill are appropriate for programs of any theme and for either age group (though you may wish to modify them for the youngest children so that "reading along" is not required).

The goals of these programs include introducing children to different literary forms (such as poetry and drama), teaching them about the library and about different kinds of books, and encouraging them to work together on projects. The children will use both mental and motor skills in these programs, and their success will help develop their sense of self-worth.

Every program in this book has been fully executed with children and librarians, and all have been enthusiastically accepted.

I hope that you will enjoy these programs and find them fun, helpful, and rewarding.

Taffy Jones

1. Library Bears

The Library Bears programs focus on poetry and drama and how they can enhance one another. Children will have the chance to write their own poetry and to produce a play. There are also opportunities to learn about fiction and nonfiction, and to see, through the study of bears, how exciting natural science can be.

Library Bears:
Grades 1–4, Long Program
Time: 4 days; 2 1/2 hours each day

FIRST DAY
Getting Started: Bear name tags (15 min.)
Story Time: Book about bears (15 min.)
Library Time: Tour the library (15 min.)
Bear Games: "Got a Bear by the Tail" (15 min.)
Bear Crafts: Color flannel-board characters (30 min.)
Washup and Snack: Graham crackers, honey, milk or juice (15 min.)
Bear Drama: "The Bear Climbed the Tree"—read-through (30 min.)
Finishing Up (15 min.)

SECOND DAY
Getting Started: Parents' Day invitations (15 min.)
Story Time: "Blueberries for Sal" (15 min.)
Library Time: Show film about bears (15 min.)
Bear Games: "The Den of the Bear" (15 min.)
Bear Crafts: Refrigerator Bear (30 min.)
Washup and Snack: Blueberry muffins, butter, Kool-aid (15 min.)
Bear Drama: "The Bear Climbed the Tree"—practice (30 min.)
Finishing Up (15 min.)

THIRD DAY
Getting Started: Name rhymes (15 min.)
Story Time: Book of poetry (15 min.)
Library Time: Talk about poetry (15 min.)
Bear Games: "Bear to Bear" (15 min.)
Bear Crafts: Roger Poet and His Bear (30 min.)
Washup and Snack: Gingerbread bears, juice (15 min.)
Bear Drama: Practice name rhymes and "The Bear Climbed the Tree" (30 min.)
Finishing Up (15 min.)

FOURTH DAY
Getting Started: Bear poetry (15 min.)
Story Time: Book of poetry (15 min.)
Bear Games: "Teddy Bears' Picnic" (15 min.)
Bear Crafts: Bear place setting (30 min.)
Washup and Snack: Bear cake, soft drink (15 min.)
Bear Drama: Present "The Bear Climbed the Tree" for Parents' Day audience
(45 min.—extra time allowed for picture-taking, etc.)
Finishing Up (15 min.)

Grades 1–4, Long Program: First Day

Materials Checklist

____ bear name tags (from this book)—have a few extra
____ yarn for bear name tags
____ white cardboard for name tag backing (optional)
____ scissors
____ paper punch
____ white glue
____ markers and crayons
____ book for Story Time
____ books with poetry
____ enlarged bear drawing for games
____ scotch tape
____ long straight pins
____ paper or fur "bear's tail"
____ blindfold
____ flannel-board (flat surface for display, covered with felt)
____ flannel-board characters (from this book)—each child will receive a
      set to color
____ graham crackers
____ butter or honey (squeeze bottle of honey works best, especially the
      bear-shaped bottle)
____ milk or fruit juice
____ paper napkins
____ paper cups
____ plastic knives (to spread honey)
____ copies of "The Bear Climbed the Tree" (from this book)
____ copies of bear drawing to be used for the Parents' Day invitations
      (from this book)

The Program

Goal

To be exposed to simple poetry, drama and songs.

3

Teddy Bear name tag

Panda name tag

Preparation

Draw or enlarge on copier the bear name tags on pages 4 and 5 and photocopy enough for each child to have one (plus a few extra). You may wish to further prepare name tags for Grades 1–2 (see "Getting Started"). Prepare a complete set of (pages 12–16) of flannel-board characters (including tree) for the librarian to use in "The Bear Climbed the Tree": draw or enlarge them, color with markers or poster paints, and cut them out. Clear plastic covering or spray-on shellac will help the characters last a long time so they can be used again. Glue sandpaper to backs (top and bottom) for sticking on felt. Also photocopy a set of characters for each child to color and cut out during Bear Crafts time. Photocopy "The Bear Climbed the Tree" script (pages 9–11), one for each child plus a few extra. Make a paper or fur "bear's tail" for the game "Got a Bear by the Tail."

Getting Started   (Two groups,* 15 minutes)

The children are divided into two groups or dens at opposite ends of the room. Tables are great, but chair seats make good tables. The floor does, too.

Grades 1–2 are the Teddy Bears and Grades 3–4 are Pandas. Give each child an appropriate name tag. The children write their names on the tags and color.

Grades 3–4 will like to make the entire name tag. It is better to have Grades 1–2 name tags cut out ahead, with holes punched and yarn put through to go over the head.

Story Time   (One group, 15 minutes)

The two bear dens join together for Story Time. They sit around the librarian's chair and the librarian reads them a book about bears. (See Bear Book List.)

Library Time   (One group, 15 minutes)

Talk about books. There are all different kinds of books: poetry books, biography books, mystery books, science books, books of fables and facts. (Explain these books.)

Read a book in rhyming verse. Discuss how it is different from a book without poetry.

---

*"Two groups" notation signifies that division of a large group is appropriate or desirable for an activity. You may prefer not to divide small groups.

Take a short Bear Tour of the library. Point out special things like the card catalog, computers, new book arrivals, etc. If group is large, divide into two groups. An assistant reads a bear or poetry book to one group while the other bears tour. Then they switch.

Bear Games   (One group, 15 minutes)

"Got a Bear by the Tail." Draw or photocopy (enlarge) a big bear picture. (The one given in this book for the flannel-board play is a good choice). Tape or tack to the wall. The children line up and the first child is given a bear's tail made of construction paper, or a piece of fur, with a long straight pin in it (warn children to handle pin carefully). Blindfold the child and spin him around, then point him in the direction of the big bear. Each child takes a turn to see who can pin the bear's tail the closest to where it belongs. (You can have each child mark the spot he hit.) The children can help along the way—"You are way off—you are getting hot." The child who comes the closest to the correct tail position is the winner.

Bear Crafts   (Two groups, 30 minutes)

Each child receives a set of photocopied flannel-board characters from the flannel-board play, "The Bear Climbed the Tree." They color the characters and cut them out. They could also use them to follow the librarian's actions in "The Bear Climbed the Tree" (optional).

Washup   (One group at a time, 5 minutes)

Teddy Bears go before Pandas. Children who finish crafts before the others may also wash up first.

Snack   (One group, 10 minutes)

Bears love honey! Serve honey-flavor or plain graham crackers with butter or honey, and milk or fruit juice.

Bear Drama   (One group, 30 minutes)

Read through the flannel-board play, "The Bear Climbed the Tree." (Readers can follow along in their scripts.) The librarian moves the characters on the flannel-board as the story directs. Children may want to hold up their own sets of characters to match what the librarian does, but this is optional; they will enjoy just watching and singing.

Finishing up (One group, 15 minutes)

Explain that the last day of the program will be Parents' Day, when parents or friends can come to see the play. Let the children take their photocopied scripts home to practice the song (parents can help non-readers). Tell the children that they will make invitations for Parents' Day next time you meet.

Collect bear name tags.

The Bear Climbed the Tree

A Flannel-board Play
by
Taffy Jones
Drawings by Lomie Helmich

BEAR
WIGGLY WORM
UGLY FROG
BUZZING BEE
FLYING BIRD
ME (two different pictures)
NARRATOR: (Librarian)
CHORUS: (Children)

Props:
flannel-board
an 18″ tree for the flannelboard

This play is sung to the tune "The Bear Went Over the Mountain." The children are the chorus. They sit in a semi-circle facing the flannel-board.

(Place the tree on the flannel-board, then start the song. Place the bear at the bottom of the tree.)

CHORUS *(Sings):*   The bear climbed the tree-e
The bear climbed the tree-e
The bear climbed the tree-eee
And guess what he did see?

NARRATOR: What?
(Moves the bear higher up the tree and adds a worm near the tree.)

CHORUS *(Sings):*   He saw a wiggly worrrrm
He was a wiggly worrrrm

9

	He saw a wiggly worrrrm
	And that is what he saw.
NARRATOR:	*(Takes away worm, moves the bear a little higher up the tree, and adds the frog near the tree.)*
CHORUS *(Sings):*	He saw an ugly fro-og
	He saw an ugly fro-og
	He saw an ugly frooo-oog
	And that is what he saw.
NARRATOR:	*(Takes frog away and adds the bee a little above the bear. The bear has been moved farther up the tree.)*
CHORUS *(Sings):*	He heard a buzzing bee-e
	He heard a buzzing bee-e
	He heard a buzzing bee-eee
	A bee he never saw
NARRATOR:	*(Takes the bee away, moves the bear up the tree, and adds the bird near the top of the tree.)*
CHORUS *(Sings):*	He saw a flying bir-rd
	He saw a flying bir-rd
	He saw a flying birr-rd
	And that is what he saw.
NARRATOR:	*(Takes bird away and puts bear at the top of the tree.)*
	(Speaks) The bear climbed to the top of the tree. Then what did he see?
CHORUS *(Sings):*	The bear saw ME-EEEEE
	The bear saw ME-EEEEE
	The bear saw ME-EEEE-EEEE
	And ME was scared as ME could be.
NARRATOR:	*(Speaks)* Then what happened?
CHORUS *(Sings):*	ME fell out the the tree-eeee
	ME fell out of the tree-eeee
	ME fell out of the tree-eeee-ee
	Because the bear growled at ME.
	GRRRRRRRRRR!
NARRATOR:	*(Speaks)* Is that the end of the story?
CHORUS:	No!
NARRATOR:	*(Have ME follow the words of the song on the flannel board)*
CHORUS *(Sings):*	ME hit the flying bir-rd
NARRATOR:	*(Takes out bird)*
CHORUS *(Sings):*	ME hit the buzzing bee-ee — ouch!

NARRATOR:	*(Takes out bee)*
CHORUS *(Sings):*	ME hit the ugly frog-og
NARRATOR:	*(Takes out the frog)*
CHORUS *(Speaks):*	ME also hit the wiggly worm!
NARRATOR:	*(Takes out worm)*
	(Speaks) What happened to ME?
	(Takes away ME and adds boy with bandages)
CHORUS *(Sings):*	ME broke his big, fat toe, (Point to toe)
	ME broke his turned-up no-ose (Point to nose)
	ME broke his knee-ees (Point to knees)
	Because ME fell out of the tree.
CHORUS *(Speaks):*	Poor ME!
NARRATOR:	*(Speaks)* What happened to the bear?
CHORUS *(Speaks):*	Don't know!
	Don't care!!
	So there!!!

The End

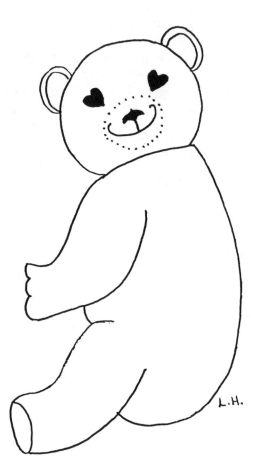

Bear

Ugly frog and wiggly worm

Buzzing bee and flying bird

Me (first picture)

Me (second picture)

Grades 1–4, Long Program: Second Day

Materials Checklist

____ bear name tags (from previous day)
____ crayons or markers
____ bears for Parents' Day invitations (from this book) — have a few extra
____ book: "Blueberries for Sal," by Robert McClosky
____ film projector
____ film about bears
____ white cardboard backing for the bears
____ varnish
____ brushes
____ small magnets (enough for each child to have one)
____ white glue
____ scissors
____ paper punch
____ blueberry muffins
____ butter
____ kool-aid
____ paper napkins
____ paper cups
____ flannel-board play script, flannel-board, characters (librarian's set)

The Program

Goal

To learn more about bears and their habits, and discover how exciting natural science books can be.

Preparation

Draw or enlarge on copier the teddy bear name tag on page 4, and photocopy enough for each child to have one (plus a few extra). Draw or reduce to a small size the same bear for refrigerator magnets; again, have one for each child plus extra.

You may wish to bake your own blueberry muffins ahead of time rather than purchasing them, or the children could bake them.

17

Getting Started (Two groups, 15 minutes)

The children are in their Bear Dens. Grades 1–2 are the Teddy Bears and grades 3–4 are the Pandas. Give out bear name tags.

Give each child a photocopied bear for a Parents' Day invitation. The children color the bears, then write on them (librarian can help):

PLACE:
DATE:
TIME:

(and fill in the appropriate information).

Story Time (One group, 15 minutes)

The children gather around the librarian for Story Time. The librarian reads "Blueberries for Sal," by Robert McClosky.

Talk about the book. Has anyone seen a real bear? Does anyone know any *true* bear stories? How many books can you name that are stories about pretend bears—fiction? ("Three Bears," "Corduroy," "Winnie the Pooh," the "Paddington Bear" books, etc.)

Library Time (One group, 15 minutes)

Show a film about real bears.

Bear Games (One group, 15 minutes)

Play "The Den of the Bear." One child is chosen to play the Library Bear. The other children turn their backs and close their eyes—no peeking! The Library Bear hides in a bear cave (any good hiding place in the room). The children count slowly to twenty. Then the children go looking for the Library Bear. Whenever someone finds the Library Bear, that person goes in the cave and hides with the Library Bear. The last child to lie down in the bear cave becomes the new Library Bear, and the game starts again.

Bear Crafts (Two groups, 30 minutes)

Make a Refrigerator Bear: Give each child a copy of the small-size bear name tag. The children color the bear and then cut it out. They make a cardboard backing for the bear and varnish the complete bear. They glue a small magnet to the back of the bear, and the bear is ready to hang on the refrigerator.

Washup   (One group at a time, 5 minutes)

The Teddy Bears, or the children who have finished their crafts, go first.

Snacks   (One group, 10 minutes)

Blueberry muffins, butter, and Kool-aid.

Bear Drama   (One group, 30 minutes)

Rehearse the flannel-board play, "The Bear Climbed the Tree." You can have some of the children take turns holding up the characters in the play.

Finishing Up   (Two groups, 15 minutes)

The children finish their Parents' Day invitations. They can make others for their friends, if they like. (Use extra copies.)

Talk about Parents' Day.

Collect bear name tags.

Grades 1–4, Long Program: Third Day

Materials Checklist

_____ bear name tags (from previous days)
_____ crayons, markers, pens or pencils
_____ scissors
_____ white glue
_____ paper for writing rhymes
_____ book selections—poetry books
_____ photocopies of Roger Poet (from this book)—one for each child
_____ photocopies of small bear for Roger Poet's teddy bear (from this book)—one for each child
_____ cardboard for framing Roger Poet—enough for frame and backing for each child (colored cardboard is a nice touch)
_____ gingerbread bears
_____ apple juice or cranberry juice
_____ paper napkins
_____ paper cups
_____ flannel-board play script, flannel-board, and characters (librarian's set)

The Program

Goal

To have fun with poetry and write rhymes.

Preparation

Photocopy "Roger Poet" on page 23 (you may wish to enlarge picture, or draw a larger version yourself). Make enough copies for each child to have one. Draw or photocopy a small bear—any bear from this book, copied in a small size, will do. (Again, have a copy for each child.) The bear should be small enough to attach to Roger Poet's hand, like a teddy bear.

Getting Started   (Two groups, 15 minutes)

The children are in their bear dens. Give out bear name tags.

The children write name rhymes. They write on a piece of paper: "My name is _____." Then have them write another sentence and the last word rhymes with their name. (You can do this with first or last names, but some last names can be quite challenging! You can make the challenge part of the game: who has the easiest name to rhyme? Who has the hardest?)

Example: My name is Cathie Brown.
              I jump up and down.

Have the children take their name (you can choose last or first—or let each child choose) and write all the words that sound like it.

Example: The last name is Brown. Go through the alphabet and find words that sound like brown: around, bound, crown, down, found, ground, gown, etc. Look for more than one word.

After you have the words, make up more name rhymes and write them down.

Story Time   (One group, 15 minutes)

The children sit around the librarian, who reads from a book of poetry, then shows them other poetry books as well.

Library Time   (One group, 15 minutes)

Help the children find and choose books of poetry on the shelves. Look over their book selections.

Talk about different kinds of poetry. For example, what is a limerick? A limerick is a short, funny poem with a rhythm about it. Lines 1, 2 and 5 rhyme and have eight to ten syllables. Lines 3 and 4 rhyme and have five to seven syllables.

Look up the meaning of the words "meter" and "measure."

What is a triplet? A triplet is a three-line poem where all the lines rhyme.

What are clerihews? Clerihews are a form of poetry based on names. Each clerihew is four lines long. The first two lines rhyme, as do the last two.

What is a couplet? A couplet is two rhyming lines.

There are some fine books on writing poetry for children. Use *Poetry Patterns* by Charla Jones, published by Book Lures Inc., P. O. Box 9450, O'Fallon, Mo. 63366, to add to your poetry sessions.

Bear Games   (One group, 15 minutes)

"Bear to Bear." The children (Library Bears) choose partners. The partners face each other, and the group is in one large circle. A bear without a

21

partner is chosen to be the Bear Leader and stands in the middle of the circle. If number of children is even, the librarian can take part—you need an odd number so there is always one person without a partner.

The Bear Leader calls, "Library Bears, Back to Back." The bears stand back to back. The Bear Leader calls, "Library Bears, Fact to Face." The bears turn fact to face.

The Bear Leader can alternate these calls as long as he or she likes; then he or she tries to surprise the Bears with, "Library Bears, change partners!" The Bears all try to find new partners, including the Bear Leader. Whoever is left without a partner is the next Bear Leader, and the game is repeated.

Bear Crafts   (Two groups, 30 minutes)

Roger Poet and His Bear. Each child has a photocopy of Roger Poet and a small bear. They color the pictures. Then they cut out the bear and Roger Poet, and glue the bear to Roger's hand. Next they glue Roger and his bear to a square of cardboard (white or any color) and cut out a cardboard frame (colored if you have it) to glue on the front.

Washup   (One group at a time, 5 minutes)

Teddy Bears, or those who finish crafts first, go first.

Snacks   (One group, 10 minutes)

Gingerbread bears (look for ready-made bear cookies, or whatever you can find), apple juice or cranberry juice.

Bear Drama   (One group, 30 minutes)

Dress rehearsal for the flannel-board play. The children practice saying their name rhymes (standing in a straight line facing the audience, they say their rhymes in turn); this is how they will open the play on Parents' Day. Then practice the play.

Finishing Up   (Two groups, 15 minutes)

Remind children about Parents' Day; tell them they can also bring friends, and that guests may take pictures if they like.

Ask children to bring a teddy bear from home for next time. If they have no teddy bear, they can bring their favorite toy or stuffed animal.

Collect bear name tags.

Roger Poet

23

Grades 1–4, Long Program: Fourth Day

Materials Checklist

____ bear name tags (from previous days)
____ pencils
____ paper
____ children's poetry books
____ tape or record of "Teddy Bear's Picnic"
____ record player or tape recorder
____ picnic basket
____ large table cloth or blanket
____ paper napkins
____ paper cups
____ cardboard (for bear placemats)
____ scissors
____ white glue
____ crayons, markers or poster paints
____ graham crackers
____ bear cake
____ soft drink
____ flannel-board play script, flannel-board, and characters (librarian's set)
____ chairs for audience
____ teddy bears or other stuffed animals (children bring from home—it's good to have a few on hand for those who forget)

The Program

Goal

To have more poetry time, and to present play for audience.

Preparation

If you wish to use any bears from this book for decorating Bear Place Settings, make as many copies as you think you will need. Set up chairs for Parents' Day audience, and have flannel-board set up, with script and characters ready on hand.

You may wish to bake a bear-shaped cake ahead of time; otherwise, any store-bought cake will do.

Getting Started   (Two groups, 15 minutes)

The children are in their bear dens. Give out name tags. Do bear poetry: Remind them how they wrote their name rhymes last time, and learned how much fun it is to write rhymes. Today they will do *bear poetry*, all about bears. Here is an example:

Buddy Bear lost his *clothes.*

He was embarrassed, goodness *knows.*

Try some more couplets. Explain how to think of words that rhyme— moon, tune; dance, pants; etc. Think of a word, then go through the alphabet to find words that rhyme. Example: BEAR: air, bare, care, dare, fair, etc. Not all letters will produce rhyming words.

Here's some more Bear Poetry:

There once was a bear named Buddy,
Whose Mom was a fuddy-duddy,
Buddy sat in a chair,
While Mom combed his hair,
And his paws were never muddy.

Which words rhyme?

One day Buddy said, "I declare,
I will not be a fuddy-duddy!
I will not comb my hair.
My jeans will have a hole in them,
And I will get real muddy."

Which line doesn't rhyme?

One day, Buddy met Betty Bear,
Betty was quite a honey,
These two would make a perfect pair,
But, Betty was out for money.
(Betty Bear didn't care for messy hair.)

Which lines have rhyming words?

But Buddy Bear loved Betty Bear,
And wanted her for his honey,
So Buddy Bear combed his hair,
And made a lot of money.

How many lines rhyme?

So, now there's a bear named Buddy,
Who is an awful fuddy-duddy,
Buddy sits in a chair,
While his wife combs his hair,
And his paws are never muddy.

Now it is your turn to write Bear Poetry. Make up a new bear and what he does, or make up some more about Buddy Bear.

When you have finished your Bear Poetry, read the poem written by poet Patrick J. Peters. Talk about his poem.

The Poetical Bear

There was a brown bear
Whose friends called him Cyd
Who loved to write poems
And that's just what he did.

He wrote poems about animals
And all about trees,
Of blueberries, honey,
And running from bees.

He wrote about flowers,
The stars in the night,
And the moon on the water,
Shining so bright.

Cyd wrote poems about friendship,
And all about love,
Of the beauty of nature,
And heaven above.

Deep in the forest
Where Cyd makes his home,
You can always find him
Writing a poem.

—*Patrick J. Peters*

Story Time   (One group, 15 minutes)

The children sit around the librarian, who reads a book of children's poems. (See Poetry Book List.)

Library Time

No library time today.

Bear Games   (One group, 15 minutes)

"Teddy Bears' Picnic." Spread a large table cloth or blanket on the floor and put a picnic basket in the center. Play a record or tape of "Teddy Bears' Picnic" while the children walk around the blanket in a large circle. They are Library Bears on a picnic. The children carry their teddy bears or stuffed animals with them. When the librarian points to a child, that child puts his or her teddy bear on the blanket with the picnic basket in the center of the circle, and then goes back into the circle. This continues until all teddy bears and animals are on the blanket. The music and walking around in the circle continues.

Now the librarian tells the Library Bears to get on their knees. A first Library Bear is chosen to start "bear jumping" (like leap frog). The first bear jumps over the next bear's back and then jumps back to where it started in the circle. The next bear repeats the bear jumping. Each child has a turn. At the end, everyone has a graham cracker and the children pick up their teddy bears. That ends "The Teddy Bears' Picnic."

Bear Crafts   (Two groups, 30 minutes)

A Bear Place Setting. Decorate paper cups, plates and napkins with bears. Decorate cardboard for bear placemats. Do as many of these place setting items as there is time. The decorations can be original drawings, or any of the bears photocopied from this book. Color the bears with poster paints or markers. Note: Decorating napkins is optional. Their texture does not always make a good surface for drawing and coloring.

Washup (One group at a time, 5 minutes)

Teddy bears, or those who finish crafts first, go first.

Snacks (One group, 10 minutes)

Bear cake and soft drink.

Bear Drama (One group, 45 minutes)

Present "The Bear Climbed the Tree" for audience. Audience can take pictures if they like. (Extra time is provided for set-up, picture-taking, etc.)

Finishing Up (Two groups, 15 minutes)

Talk about the bear program and bear poetry. Is there anyone who would really like to be a poet? Anyone who would like to be a writer?

Tell the children they were great Library Bears, and ask them to come back soon.

Children take home bear name tags, crafts, poems, etc.

Library Bears:
Grades 1–4, Short Program
Time: 2 days; 1 1/2 hours each day

Getting Started: Bear name tags (10 min.)
Story Time: Book of children's poetry (10 min.)
Library Time: Talk about poetry; short tour of library (10 min.)
Bear Games: "The Bears Went Over the Mountain" (5 min.)
Bear Crafts: Bear Visor (15 min.)
Washup and Snack: Frosted bear cookies, milk (15 min.)
Bear Drama: "A Bear Poetry Play"—read through (20 min.)
Finishing Up (5 min.)

SECOND DAY
Getting Started: (5 min.)
Story Time: Book about bears (15 min.)
Library Time: Sleuthing Out the Card Catalog (10 min.)
Bear Games: "Dancing Bears" (5 min.)
Bear Crafts: Teddy Bear paper doll (15 min.)
Washup and Snack: Teddy Bear grahams, apple juice (15 min.)
Bear Drama: Present "A Bear Poetry Play" for Parents' Day Audience (20 min.)
Finishing Up (5 min.)

Grades 1–4, Short Program: First Day

Materials Checklist

____ bear name tags (from this book)—have a few extra
____ yarn for name tags
____ crayons or markers
____ scissors
____ white glue
____ poetry books
____ stapler
____ paper punch
____ pattern for Bear Visor (from this book)—on heavy cardboard
____ construction paper
____ pencils
____ paper
____ bear cookies
____ milk
____ paper napkins
____ paper cups
____ copies of "A Bear Poetry Play" (from this book)—have a few extra
____ props for play: 2 chairs, big towel, safety pin, apron, comb

The Program

Goal

Adding poetry to drama.

Preparation

Draw or enlarge on copier the bear name tags on pages 4 and 5 and photocopy enough for each child to have one (plus a few extra). You may wish to further prepare name tags for Grades 1–2 (see "Getting Started"). Photocopy script for "A Bear Poetry Play" (pages 36–37)—have a few extra. Enlarge the bear visor patterns (visor, band, and teddy bear) on pages 34–35 and trace them on heavy cardboard, then cut out.

Getting Started   (Two groups,* 10 minutes)

The children are divided into two groups or dens at opposite ends of the room (at tables or on floor).

Grades 1–2 are Teddy Bears and Grades 3–4 are Pandas. Give each child an appropriate name tag. The children write their names on the tags and color.

Grades 3–4 will have to make the entire name tag. It is better to have Grades 1–2 name tags cut out ahead, with holes punched and yarn put through to go over the head.

Story Time   (One group, 10 minutes)

The children sit around the librarian, who reads them a book of poems. (See Poetry Book List.)

Library Time   (Two groups, 10 minutes)

Talk about poetry.

Talk about rhyming their names with rhyming words. Try it. *Example:* My name is Billy *Brown*. I am the finest boy in *town*. (You can do this with first or last names.)

Think of other words that rhyme with their names. *Example:* BROWN— town, sound, down, mound, found, ground, etc. Go through the alphabet and find the words that rhyme with your name.

Talk about a limerick. A limerick is a very funny, short poem that rhymes in a pattern: The first, second, and fifth lines rhyme, and the third and fourth rhyme. Example:

There once was a bear named Buddy.
Whose Mom was a fuddy-duddy.
Buddy sat in his chair,
While Mom combed his hair,
And Buddy Bear never got muddy.

Now try to write a limerick. Start with what you already have:

*"Two groups" notation signifies that division of a large group is appropriate or desirable for an activity. You may prefer not to divide small groups.

Library Bears

> My name is Billy Brown.
> I am the finest boy in town.
> I wash my face,
> I'm not a disgrace,
> And I'm nice to have around.

Look up poetry books and show them. Read a couple of poems.

Take a short tour of the library. If group is large, divide into two groups. While one group is touring, some poems are read to the others.

Bear Games   (One group, 5 minutes)

"The Bears Went Over the Mountain." The children are the bears and they sing to the tune, "The Bear Went Over the Mountain," as they walk around the room.

> Oh, the bears went over the mountain,
> The bears went over the mountain,
> The bears went over the mountain,
> To see what they could see.

The children stop walking. They put their hands to their eyes and look all around. They saw—

> The other side of the mountain,
> The other side of the mountain,
> The other side of the mountain,
> Was all that they could see—and—
> We saw a _____.

A child calls out what they saw. Example: "A frog." The child hops around like a frog.

> We saw a frog,
> We saw a frog,
> We saw a frog . . .

At this point you can fill in a rhyming line, even one that suggests an action—for example, "And the frog fell off the log" (and the frog falls down). If you can't think of a rhyme, just sing:

> And that is what they saw.

32

Bear Crafts   (Two groups, 15 minutes)

Bear Visors. Using the bear visor pattern from this book, the librarian helps the children trace the pattern on heavy construction paper, any color. (The children pick out their color, if a variety is available.) The children cut out the brims and bands and staple the bands to the brims. The librarian helps the children measure enough elastic to go around their heads (about 12″ – add or subtract for head sizes). Then the children staple elastic to their visors.

Now the librarian can help children trace the teddy bear (pages 34–35) on construction paper or felt. They cut it out and glue it to the middle of the visor brim.

The children will love wearing visors. They can add their names and have other children sign their names to the visor; or some will prefer to keep the visor plain, with only the teddy bear.

Washup   (One group at a time, 5 minutes)

Teddy Bears go before Pandas; or those who have finished crafts may wash up first.

Snacks   (One group, 10 minutes)

Frosted bear cookies and milk. (There are bags of bear cookies already frosted in the grocery stores.)

Bear Drama   (One group, 20 minutes)

Read through the play "A Bear's Poetry Play." Choose who will play the characters. Do the play with the characters.

Finishing Up   (Two groups, 5 minutes)

Talk about bears, bear poetry.

Tell the children and parents about Parents' Day, which will be the next day the group meets. Parents or friends can come to see the play. Let the children take their photocopied scripts home to practice the Bear Poetry Play (parents can help non-readers).

Collect bear name tags.

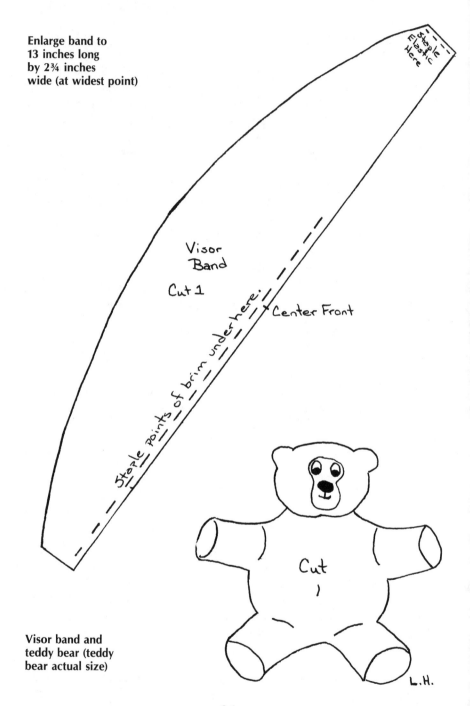

Enlarge band to
13 inches long
by 2¾ inches
wide (at widest point)

Staple
Elastic
Here

Visor
Band

Cut 1

Staple points of brim under here.

Center Front

Cut
1

Visor band and
teddy bear (teddy
bear actual size)

L.H.

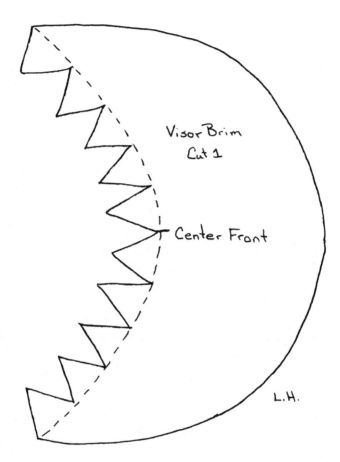

Visor Brim
Cut 1

Center Front

L.H.

Visor brim: enlarge to 8¼ inches long by 6⅛ inches wide at widest point.

35

A Bear Poetry Play
by
Taffy Jones

Characters:

BUDDY BEAR
BETTY BEAR
MOM BEAR
POEM TELLER (Librarian)
LIBRARY BEARS (Children)

Props:

2 chairs
big towel
safety pin
comb
apron

The play takes place in Buddy Bear's kitchen. Mom Bear (who wears an apron) is combing Buddy Bear's hair. Buddy is wearing a big towel around his neck (*loosely* pinned with a safety pin). The Library Bears are seated on the floor around Buddy's chair. The Poem Teller sits in a chair to one side of the scene.

POEM TELLER:	Today, we are going to tell you the story of Buddy Bear in a Bear Poetry Play. Buddy Bear is seated in a chair in his kitchen, and Mom Bear is combing his hear.
POEM TELLER:	There once was a bear named Buddy.
LIBRARY BEARS:	There once was a bear named Buddy.
POEM TELLER:	Whose Mom was a fuddy-duddy.
LIBRARY BEARS:	Fuddy duddy. Fuddy duddy.
POEM TELLER:	Buddy sat in a chair, While his Mom combed his hair.
LIBRARY BEARS:	She's got ya, Buddy.
POEM TELLER:	And his paws were never muddy.
LIBRARY BEARS:	Clean bear. Clean bear.

POEM TELLER:	One day Buddy said, "I declare..."
BUDDY BEAR:	*(Jumps up and tears off the towel and throws it on the floor)* I will NOT be a fuddy duddy, I will NOT comb my hair. *(Shakes head no)* So there! So there! *(Sticks out his tongue.)* And I will get my paws all muddy. *(Stomps around)*
LIBRARY BEARS:	You tell 'em, Buddy.
POEM TELLER:	One day, Buddy Bear met Betty Bear.
BETTY BEAR:	*(Enters walking like a slick, chic bear)*
LIBRARY BEARS:	*(With honey voices)* Hello, Betty.
POEM TELLER:	Betty was quite a honey.
LIBRARY BEARS:	*(In honey voices)* Hello, Honey.
POEM TELLER:	These two bears make a perfect pair, But, Betty was out for money. Betty didn't care for messy hair. So she wouldn't be his honey. But, Buddy Bear *loved* Betty Bear, And wanted her for his honey, So Buddy Bear combed his hair, And made a lot of money.
LIBRARY BEARS:	Fat bear. Rich bear.
BUDDY BEAR:	*(Struts his stuff)*
POEM TELLER:	So, now there is a bear named Buddy, Who is an awful fuddy duddy.
LIBRARY BEARS:	Oh, no! Say it's not so.
POEM TELLER:	Buddy sits in a chair.
BUDDY BEAR:	*(Sits in the chair)*
POEM TELLER:	While his wife combs his hair, And his feet are never muddy.
LIBRARY BEARS:	Oh, Fuddy. Oh, Duddy. Oh, Buddy.
POEM TELLER:	The End.

The End

Grades 1–4, Short Program: Second Day

Materials Checklist

____ bear name tags (from previous day)
____ books about bears—one fiction, one nonfiction
____ record or tape for bear dancing
____ record or tape player
____ teddy bear paper doll and clothes (from this book)—have a few extra
____ teddy bear grahams
____ apple juice
____ paper cups
____ paper napkins
____ script for "A Bear Poetry Play" (for librarian)
____ props for play: 2 chairs, big towel, safety pin, apron, comb
____ make-up (if desired)
____ cleansing cream (for removal of make-up)
____ tissues
____ scissors
____ white glue
____ markers and crayons
____ photocopy the card catalog

The Program

Goals

To have the children work together; to think about one of nature's animals; and to learn about the card catalog.

Preparation

Photocopy "Sleuthing Out the Card Catalog," page 43—enough for group. Photocopy the teddy bear paper doll, pages 39–41—enough copies for the group, plus a few extra. Set up chairs for audience for "A Bear Poetry Play" (pages 36-37).

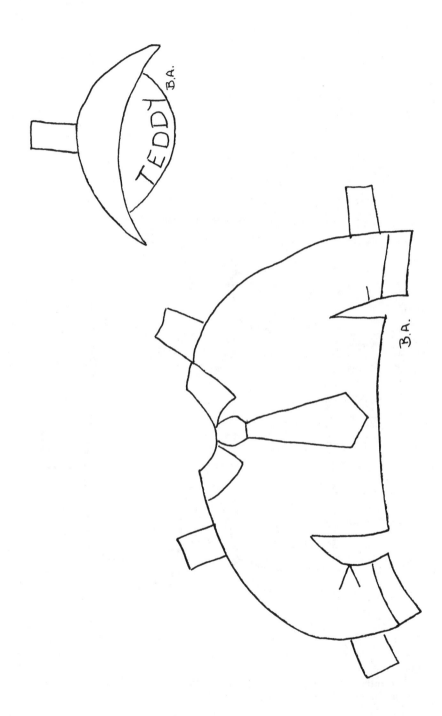

TEDDY B.A.

B.A.

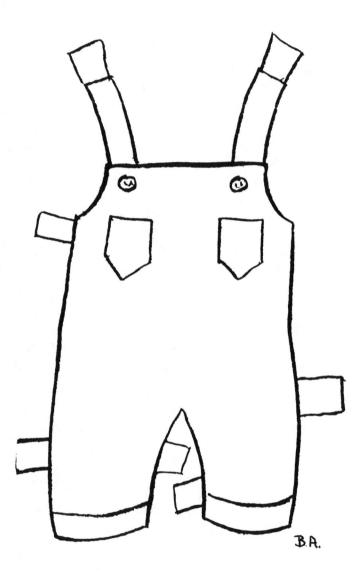

Here and previous page: clothes for Teddy Bear paper doll. Next page: Teddy Bear paper doll. (Doll and clothes actual size.)

B.A.

Getting Started (Two groups, 5 minutes)

The Teddy Bears and the Pandas are in their bear dens. Give out bear name tags.

Story Time (One group, 15 minutes)

The children sit around the librarian, who reads them two bear books. One story is a picture book story—fiction—and the other is a story about real bears—natural history. Talk about fiction and nonfiction books.

Library Time (One group, 10 minutes)

Pass out copies of "Sleuthing Out the Card Catalog," and go over them with the children, standing around the card catalog, showing them examples as you go. (Move to the shelves for discussion of call number, if you like.)

Bear Games (One group, 5 minutes)

"Bear Dancing." Put on a lively record or tape. The Library Bears dance to the music. The librarian calls out random instructions: "Dance with a partner." "Dance alone." "Spin on the floor." "Jump up." "Dance with two bears." "Dance with three bears." "Dance with four bears." "All bears dance together." "All bears fall down."

Bear Crafts (Two groups, 20 minutes)

Teddy Bear Paper Dolls. Each child receives a photocopied teddy bear and teddy clothes to color. Cut out Teddy and his clothes. (Remember, do not cut the tabs on the clothes.) A cardboard backing may be added to the teddy bear to make it more durable.

Washup (One group at a time, 5 minutes)

The Pandas follow the Teddy Bears; or those who have finished crafts may wash up first.

Snacks (One group, 10 minutes)

Teddy bear grahams, apple juice.

Sleuthing Out the Card Catalog

The card catalog is an alphabetical card file containing **author, title** and **subject** cards. You can use it to look up books in three ways.

▶ **Find the author.** Look in the card catalog under the author's last name. Example: Look in the "A" drawer to find a card for the author Pamela Allen.

▶ **Find the title.** Look for the first work in a book's title, unless the first word is "A," "An," or "The"—in that case, look for the *second* word. Example: Look in the "B" drawer to find Pamela Allen's *Berite and the Bear*.

▶ **Find the subject.** Look up the subject. Example: To find books on the subject of bears, look in the "B" drawer under "Bears." To find a book about Daniel Boone, look in the "B" drawer under "Boone, Daniel" (when looking up a person, always look for the *last* name).

Every catalog card contains a *call number* in its upper left corner. The call number tells where the book may be found on the library shelf.

Non-fiction books are shelved in order by number from 000 to 999 and under each number alphabetically by the author's name. Example: 531 D is shelved before 532 A, and 641 A comes before 641 C.

Fiction books are arranged on the shelf alphabetically by the author's last name.

Bear Drama (One group, 20 minutes)

Present "A Bear Poetry Play" for audience. Audience can take pictures. Your Bears may enjoy wearing simple make-up. If so, have helpers for children in putting on and taking off make-up. (Have cleansing cream and tissues on hand.) Example: Black noses, dark eyebrows.

Finishing Up (One group, 5 minutes)

Talk about writing and poetry. Talk about the bear program.

Tell the children they have been great Library Bears, and ask them to come back to the library soon.

Children take home crafts, name tags, etc.

Library Bears:
Preschool–Kindergarten, Long Program
Time: 2 days; 1 1/2 hours each day

FIRST DAY
Getting Started: Bear name tags (10 min.)
Story Time: Book about bears (10 min.)
Library Time: Library talk; short tour of library (10 min.)
Bear Games: "Bouncing Bears" (5 min.)
Bear Crafts: Paper Bears (15 min.)
Washup and Snack: Peanut butter with honey on crackers, milk (15 min.)
Bear Drama: "A Bear Poetry Play" or "The Bear Climbed the Tree"—
read-through (20 min.)
Finishing Up: (5 min.)

SECOND DAY
Getting Started: Color bear climbing tree (5 min.)
Story Time: Book about bears (10 min.)
Library Time: Talk about poetry; show poetry books (10 min.)
Bear Games: Bear story with actions (5 min.)
Bear Crafts: Bear Banners (15 min.)
Washup and Snack: Bear brownies, canned fruit punch (15 min.)
Bear Drama: Present "A Bear Poetry Play" or "The Bear Climbed the Tree" (20 min.)
Finishing Up (5 min.)

Preschool and Kindergarten, Long Program: First Day

Materials Checklist

____ bear name tags (from this book)—have a few extra
____ yarn for name tags
____ scissors
____ stapler
____ paper punch
____ white glue
____ white cardboard for name tag backing (optional)
____ crayons and markers
____ book for Story Time
____ large ball
____ construction paper for paper bears—any color
____ paper bear pattern (from this book)
____ peanut butter
____ crackers
____ milk
____ knife (to spread peanut butter)
____ copies of scripts for "A Bear Poetry Play" or "The Bear Climbed the Tree" (from this book)
____ props for "A Bear Poetry Play" or flannel-board and characters for "The Bear Climbed the Tree" (see checklist on page 9 or 36)

The Program

Goals

To think about books, get acquainted with the library, and work together producing a play.

Preparation

Draw or enlarge on copier the bear name tag on pages 4 and 5 and photocopy enough for each child to have one (plus a few extra). Cut them out, punch holes in top, and thread yarn through the hole for wearing around neck. (Optional: add cardboard backing for strength.) Photocopy scripts of the play of your choice—"A Bear Poetry Play," pp. 36–37, or "The Bear Climbed the Tree," pp. 9–11. (Copy enough for each child to have one. The children will take these scripts home for an adult to read aloud to help them with memorization.) If you decide to do "The Bear Climbed the Tree," prepare a complete set of flannel-board characters (see "Preparation" on page 6). For Bear Crafts, photocopy the Paper Bear pattern on page 48. You may wish to do most of the folding and cutting for this craft in advance.

Getting Started   (Two groups,* 10 minutes)

The children are in groups or bear dens at opposite ends of the room. Use tables, or let the children sit on the floor and use chair seats for tables.

Give each child a bear name tag to color.

Story Time   (One group, 10 minutes)

The children sit around the librarian, who reads a book about bears, fact or fiction. (See Bear Book List.)

Library Time   (One or two groups, 10 minutes)

Talk about things in the library. See how many things can be named that pertain to the library. **OR:** The children are divided into two groups. First one side says an object in the library, then the other side says one. The side whose player can't think of an object causes that team to be out.

Take a short tour of the library, pointing out some of the things mentioned. If a large group, divide and let one group tour while the other has a bear or poetry story read to them.

---

*"Two groups" notation signifies that division of a large group is appropriate or desirable for an activity. You may prefer not to divide small groups.

Bear Games   (One group, 5 minutes)

"Bouncing Bears." The children sit in a large circle. They pass the ball from one to the other. When it reaches where it started, that bear rolls the ball across to someone on the other side of the circle. That person rolls the ball back. If any bear fails to catch the ball at any time, he or she must go into the center of the circle and either bounce the ball or toss it into the air five times. Then the game of passing or rolling the ball is resumed.

Bear Crafts   (Two groups, 15 minutes)

Make Paper Bears. Fold 8½ x 11" sheets of construction paper into six sections each, accordion-style, as shown below (folding right edge under to begin):

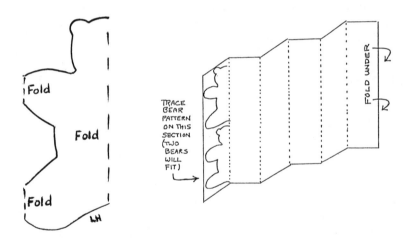

Trace Paper Bear pattern on top section of folded paper and cut out, being careful not to cut the folds. You should get two sets of three connected bears from each sheet of paper.

The children draw in the bear faces and paws. They add bows, ties, collars, necklaces, glasses, hair ribbons, etc. They can name each bear, and the librarian can help them write the names on the bears.

48

Washup
(One group at a time, 5 minutes)

The children who have finished their paper bears go first.

Snacks
(One group, 10 minutes)

Spread peanut butter on crackers, saltines or any other cracker, and add honey. (Try to find the honey bottles shaped like bears.) Serve with milk.

Bear Drama
(One group, 15 minutes)

Read through "A Bear Poetry Play." Choose the characters and act out the play. Or do "The Bear Climbed the Tree."

Finishing Up
(One group, 5 minutes)

Explain that the next day you meet will be Parents' Day, when parents and friends can come to see the play; and take pictures if they like. Let the children take home photocopies of the play scripts so parents can read aloud and help memorize.

Collect bear name tags.

Preschool–Kindergarten, Long Program: Second Day

Materials Check List

____ bear name tags (from previous day)
____ bear climbing tree (picture from this book)—one for each child (have extra)
____ book for Story Time
____ poetry books
____ crayons and markers
____ scissors
____ white glue
____ construction paper
____ copies of "A Bear Poetry Play" or "The Bear Climbed the Tree" (from this book)
____ tissues
____ brownies or cookies
____ fruit punch
____ paper napkins
____ paper cups

The Program

Goals

To talk and learn about poetry, and to present a play for audience.

Preparation

Cut pieces of construction paper into flag (triangle) or banner shapes. Set up chairs for Parents' Day audience; have either the flannel-board characters or props for "A Bear Poetry Play" ready on hand.

You may wish to bake brownies ahead of time and perhaps cut them out with a bear-shaped cutter; or, any bakery brownies will do.

Getting Started   (Two groups, 10 minutes)

The children are in their bear dens. Give out bear name tags from previous day, and photocopied picture of bear climbing the tree. The children color the picture.

Story Time   (One group, 10 minutes)

The librarian reads a bear story. (See Bear Book List.)

Library Time   (One group, 10 minutes)

Talk about poetry. Show some poetry books and read a few poems. Tell the children they can learn to write their own poems. Show them how to rhyme their names. Example: "My name is Ronnie Jones." Find a word that rhymes with the last name. (Bones, cones, phones, loans, moans.) The librarian can choose a few names and help each one chosen with the rhyming word, if the children cannot think up a rhyming word. If last names are too hard, use first names.

Bear Games   (One group, 5 minutes)

Read a bear story. When certain words are said in the story, the children clap their hands. Example: Whenever the word "bear" is said, the children clap their hands. Add another word. Example: Whenever the word "the" is said, the children stamp their feet. Add other words and actions.

Bear Crafts   (Two groups, 15 minutes)

Bear Banners. The children use the construction paper shapes (cut by librarian) to make their own bear banners. Stickers, or bear drawings reduced from this book, can be added. The children can also draw their own bears, designs and lettering. The older children can cut their own banners.

Washup   (One group at a time, 5 minutes)

The children who are finished with the crafts first, go first.

Snacks   (One group, 10 minutes)

Bear brownies (or cookies) and canned fruit punch.

Bear Drama   (One group, 20 minutes)

Present either "A Bear Poetry Play" or "The Bear Climbed the Tree."

Finishing Up   (One group, 5 minutes)

Talk about library cards. How many of the group have one? Tell the children how to get one. Show them a library card.

Ask what they liked best in the bear program.

Tell the children they have been great Library Bears. Remind them the library is for them, and to come again.

Children take home crafts, bear name tags.

Preschool–Kindergarten, Short Program
Time: 1 day; 1 1/2 hours

Getting Started: Bear name tags (10 min.)
Story Time: Book about bears (10 min.)
Library Time: Show poetry books; rhyming last names; short tour of library (10 min.)
Bear Games: "Three Bear Chairs" (5 min.)
Bear Crafts: Teddy Bear Paper Doll (15 min.)
Washup and Snack: Bear honey grahams, chocolate milk (15 min.)
Bear Drama: "A Bear Poetry Play"—read together (20 min.)
Finishing Up (5 min.)

Materials Checklist

____ bear name tags (from this book)—one for each child, but have a few extra
____ yarn for name tags
____ paper punch
____ white cardboard for name tag and paper doll backing (optional)
____ crayons and markers
____ scissors
____ white glue
____ book selections (for Story Time, Library Time)
____ teddy bear paper doll and clothes (from this book)—have a few extra
____ bear honey grahams
____ chocolate milk
____ paper cups
____ paper napkins
____ script for "A Bear Poetry Play" (copy for librarian only)
____ props for play: 2 chairs, big towel, safety pin, apron, comb
____ chairs
____ record or tape of lively music such as "Teddy Bear's Picnic"
____ record or tape player

The Program

Goals

To acquaint children with the library; to work together with other children, to be exposed to poetry, and to find that books can be shared with television. The parents may attend the play reading, if parent participation is decided upon.

Preparation

Draw or enlarge on copier the bear name tag on page 4. Make enough copies for each child to have one (plus a few extra). For this age group it is best also to cut them out, punch a hole in the top of each, and thread yarn through each hole for hanging tag around neck. Photocopy teddy bear paper doll and clothes (pages 39–41)—enough for each child, plus extra. Make one copy of script for "A Bear Poetry Play" (pages 36–37), or use book.

Getting Started   (Two groups,* 10 minutes)

The children are in their bear dens (table or floor). They color their bear name tags. The librarian can help them write their names on the front of the tags. Then the children can give a name to the bear tag itself, and the librarian can help them write these names on the back.

Story Time   (One group, 10 minutes)

The children sit around the librarian, who reads a book about bears. (See Bear Book List.)

Library Time   (One group, 10 minutes)

Read a book of poems. (See Poetry Book List.)

Have the children say their names. *Example:* "My name is Ronnie Jones." Then find a word that rhymes with the last name. (*Example:* Bones, cones, phones, loans, moans.) Make a couplet: "My name is Ronnie Jones,

*"Two groups" notation signifies that division of a large group is appropriate or desirable for an activity. You may prefer not to divide smaller groups.

and my body is full of bones." The librarian can choose a few names and help each one chosen with the rhyming word, if the children cannot think up a rhyming word. If last names are too hard, use first names.

Take a short tour of the library. If a larger number of children, take the tour in two groups. An assistant reads a story to the group not touring.

Bear Games   (One group, 5 minutes)

"Three Bear Chairs." Set up three chairs. The children form a circle around the chairs. Start the music and have the children walk around the chairs as the music plays. When the music stops (which should be suddenly), the children try to be first to sit in the chairs. The three who do get seats are the Three Bears—the winners. They step outside the circle. The game continues until all have sat in the three bear chairs.

Bear Crafts   (Two groups, 15 minutes)

Teddy Bear Paper Doll. Each child receives a copy of the teddy bear paper doll and his clothes. The children color them and cut them out. Remind them not to cut off the tabs on the clothes.

Washup   (One group, 5 minutes)

The children who have finished their crafts first, go first.

Snacks   (One group, 10 minutes)

Bear honey grahams and chocolate milk. (There are bear honey grahams available in stores.)

Bear Drama   (One group, 20 minutes)

Read "A Bear Poetry Play" and choose the characters. Read the play again helping the characters act out their parts. (Because few of the group will be readers, you will need to modify the actions so the characters don't have to read scripts.) The parents may be asked to see the play.

Finishing Up   (One group, 5 minutes)

Tell the children what great Library Bears they have been, and ask them to come again.

Tell the children to share a book with television.

Children take home teddy bear paper dolls, name tags, etc.

2. Library Mice

"Mice" who come to your library will have an adventure with mystery stories—they may even discover that reading a good mystery is as much fun as watching one on TV! Games and mystery stories will sharpen their observation skills and imaginations. The children will also learn to work together while producing a play.

Library mice show off their mouse ears and make-up. (see pages 72 and 74.)

Library Mice:
Grades 1–4, Long Program
Time: 4 days; 2 1/2 hours each day

Getting Started: Mouse name tags, Mouse money (15 min.)
Story Time: Book about mice (15 min.)
Library Time: Talk about library, mystery books; tour the library (15 min.)
Mice Games: "Mystery Word Game" (15 min.)
Mice Crafts: Mouse Stickpuppets (30 min.)
Washup and Snack: Cheese spread on crackers, fruit punch (15 min.)
Mice Drama: "Cat Attack"—read-through (30 min.)
Finishing Up (15 min.)

SECOND DAY
Getting Started: Parents' Day invitations (15 min.)
Story Time: Read "The Bank of Cheese Who-Done-It Caper" (15 min.)
Library Time: Talk about mystery stories (15 min.)
Mice Crafts: Mouse Ears and Mouse Make-Up (30 min.)
Mice Games: "Three Blind Mice" (15 min.)
Washup and Snack: Popcorn, lemonade (15 min.)
Mice Drama: "Cat Attack"—practice (30 min.)
Finishing Up (15 min.)

THIRD DAY
Getting Started: "The Cat Attack Song" (15 min.)
Story Time: Book about mice or cats (15 min.)
Library Time: Film about mice or cats, or mystery film (15 min.)
Mice Games: "Cat and Mouse Game" (15 min.)
Mice Crafts: Mouse Shopping Bags (30 min.)
Washup and Snack: Apple and cheese slices, apple juice (15 min.)
Mice Drama: "Cat Attack"—dress rehearsal (30 min.)
Finishing Up (15 min.)

FOURTH DAY
Getting Started: "The Cat Attack Ditty" (15 min.)
Story Time: Book about mice or cats (15 min.)
Mice Games: "Mice Dancing" (15 min.)
Mice Crafts: Wee Mouse (30 min.)
Washup and Snack: Cupcakes with mice faces, soft drink (15 min.)
Mice Drama: Present "Cat Attack" for Parents' Day audience
(45 min.—extra time allowed for makeup, picture-taking, etc.)
Finishing Up (15 min.)

Grades 1–4, Long Program: First Day

Materials Checklist

____ mouse name tags (from this book) – have a few extra
____ yarn for mouse name tags
____ white cardboard for name tag backing (optional)
____ scissors
____ paper punch
____ white glue
____ mouse money (from this book) – each child receives a bill
____ crayons or markers
____ book for Story Time
____ pattern for mouse stickpuppets (from this book)
____ felt
____ 9″ dowel rods
____ styrofoam eggs (medium)
____ paints, including grey acrylic
____ cotton balls
____ cardboard (for puppet ears)
____ roly-poly eyes for puppets (optional)
____ cheese spread
____ crackers
____ knife for spreading cheese spread
____ fruit punch
____ paper napkins
____ paper cups
____ script for play "Cat Attack" (one for each child)
____ props for "Cat Attack": see page 67.

The Program

Goal

To have an adventure with mystery stories.

Preparation

Photocopy mouse name tags (pages 62 and 63), enough for each child to have one (plus a few extra). You may wish to further prepare name tags for Grades 1–2 (see "Getting Started"). Photocopy mouse money (page 64)—one for each child. Enlarge (by hand or on copier) the mouse stick-puppet pattern on page 65; trace onto sturdy paper or cardboard and cut out (just one is needed.) Photocopy "Cat Attack" script (pages 67–70), one for each child (plus extra if you think you'll need them).

Getting Started   (Two groups,* 15 minutes)

The children are divided into two groups or mouse circles at opposite ends of the room. Grades 1–2 are the Country Mice and Grades 3–4 are the City Mice. Photocopied mouse name tags are given to each group. The children write their names on their name tags, or the librarian can write the names ahead of time from the sign-up sheet.

The mice drawings can be traced onto cardboard, which is then cut out and pasted to the name tag to stengthen it (optional). Children color the mice name tags. A hole is punched in the top of the mice drawing for yarn to go through. Tie the yarn long enough to go over the head.

It may work best if Grades 1–2 have help, or their name tags are made out ahead so that the children only write their names and color. Grades 3–4 will like making the entire name tag. Black markers will make the names stand out.

Make Mice Money: Hand out copies of Mice Money from this book. The children color the money and then cut it out. Then they can draw their own, and make as many bills as time permits.

Story Time   (One group, 15 minutes)

The two mice groups join together for Story Time. They sit around the librarian's chair. The librarian reads a book about mice. (See Mice and Cats Book List.)

Library Time   (One group, 15 minutes)

Talk about the library. Talk about things in the library such as the card catalog, a library card, the book stacks, and what kind of books there are

---

*"Two groups" notation signifies that division of a large group is appropriate or desirable. You may prefer not to divide small groups.

in the library. Talk about mystery books. Show where some mystery books are in the stacks.

Take a tour of the library. If group is large, divide into two groups. The group which is not touring are read another mouse or detective story.

Mice Games   (One group, 15 minutes)

"Mystery Word Game." The children are seated in a circle. Have them think of words that they might see in a mystery story. Go around the circle so each child has a turn to call one out. Write them down. If children are stuck, the librarian can hint at or suggest some of the following words:

detective	clues	plot
money	spy glass	ghosts
sidekick	badge	search
commit	fire	beat
spies	robbers	sneak-thief
cover-up	lie detector	questioning
crime	pull over	who-done-it
robbery	puzzling	track down
fingerprint	court	solve
haunt	jail	got ya
arrest	murder	line-up
suspect	guilty	not guilty
court	police	bust
hide	pardon	poison

You can also divide the group into teams and see which team thinks of the most words.

Mice Crafts   (Two groups, 30 minutes)

Mouse Stickpuppets. Trace the mouse stickpuppet pattern from page 65. Draw on felt and cut out. Remember there are two pieces, front and back, and the felt is folded at the top, not cut. Only cut out the neck.

Glue a roll of felt on a dowel at the shoulders to fill out the top of the dress. Glue a styrofoam egg (medium) on top of dowel. When the glue is dry, paint egg with grey acrylic paint. Cut out ears from the pattern on cardboard. Paint ears grey (optional). Paint inner ears a lighter color. Slit egg and glue ears in the slits. For eyes, either glue on black and white eyes or use push-in roly eyes. Draw mouth, nose and whiskers with a black marker. Glue a cotton ball on for a nose.

Country mouse name tag

62

City mouse name tag

Mouse money

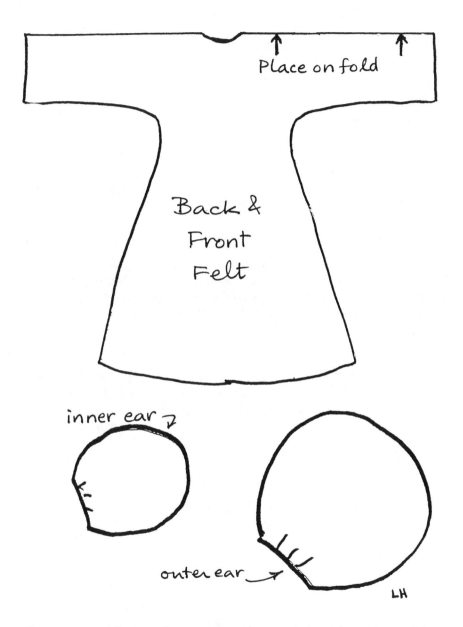

Above: Mouse stickpuppet dress pattern; enlarge to 7″ by 6″ long. Mouse stick-puppet ear patterns shown actual size.

Put the felt dress or tunic on the mouse stickpuppet. Add a ½" x 2¼" felt strip around the neck and glue. Add a ½" x 6" strip of felt for a belt. Glue a felt tail to the middle of the mouse outfit. Cut hands from cardboard and glue to ends of arms. Drawing below depicts finished stickpuppet.

Washup   (One group at a time, 5 minutes)

The Country Mice go before the City Mice, or the children who finish crafts first, go first.

Snack   (One group, 10 minutes)

Cheese spread on crackers, fruit punch.

Mice Drama   (One group, 30 minutes)

Read through the play "Cat Attack." Assign parts to the children.

Note that there are two songs in the play: "We're Smart Mice" and "The Cat Attack Ditty." These will be taught on the second and third day of the session, respectively. Leave them out for this practice.

Finishing Up   (Two groups, 15 minutes)

Explain that the last day of the program will be Parents' Day, when parents or friends can come to see the play. Let the children take the photocopied scripts home to learn their parts (parents can help non-readers). Tell the children you will make invitations for Parents' Day next time you meet.

Collect mice name tags.

Cat Attack

A Library Mouse Play
by
Taffy Jones

Characters:

LIBRARIAN MOUSE (adult)
C-A-T CAT (adult)
CHEEZER
LITTLE BITS
LIBRARY MICE

Props:

book with *Cat Attack* on cover
chairs in a straight line facing the audience
mouse books (selected from library—one for each student)
mouse ears and mouse make-up (black noses and whiskers, blue eye-shadow)
black fur cat hood, paws and tail (a full cat suit if you have it, or dark clothes or black leotards)
cat make-up (black nose and whiskers and heavy eyebrows)
mouse tails (cotton cord or rope dyed black, or black cardboard)

The children are the Library Mice. They wear large cardboard yellow (optional color) ears. Black noses and whiskers are made with black eyebrow pencil.

A row of chairs is placed facing the audience. The children enter, carrying their mouse books. They sing, "*We're Smart Mice.*" They stand in front of their chairs. The chair in the middle is for the Librarian Mouse. Librarian Mouse enters at the end of the song. She also wears mouse ears and mouse make-up. She carries a book called *Cat Attack*.

LIBRARIAN MOUSE:	It is nice to see all you Library Mice here in our library today. You have been busy mice. Will you show me the books you chose from the library?
LIBRARY MICE:	(*They hold their mouse books high.*) We like books. We like mystery books.
LIBRARIAN MOUSE:	Because you have been such good little mice, I will read you the latest thriller, hot off the press. It is called *Cat Attack.*
LIBRARY MICE:	EEEEEEEEEK! CAT ATTACK? EEEEEEEEEEK!
LIBRARIAN MOUSE:	If you will be seated, I will begin this exciting mystery.
LIBRARY MICE:	(*They sit in their chairs. Cheezer sits next to the Librarian.*)
LIBRARIAN MOUSE	(*Sits in her chair and opens the book.*) Cat Attack. This is a super mystery. It is on the Best Mystery Book List. Once upon a time, there was a big, black, furry cat. His name was C-A-T Cat. This great, handsome cat liked to gobble up Library Mice.
LIBRARY MICE:	EEEEEEEEK! Not meeeeeee!
LIBRARIAN MOUSE:	C-A-T Cat prowled around the Cheese Library looking for Library Mice to gobble up in one bite.
LIBRARY MICE:	EEEEEEEEK! Not meeeeeee! Please!!!
CHEEZER:	Are there any c-c-c-cats prowling around in our library?
LIBRARIAN MOUSE:	There are no cats prowling around in our library.
CHEEZER:	Are you sure?
LIBRARIAN MOUSE:	Yes, Cheezer, I am sure. Remember, this is only a story I am reading. Shall I go on reading?
LIBRARY MICE:	Pleeeeeeeease.
LIBRARIAN MOUSE:	C-A-T Cat saw some Library Mice sitting together, listening to a story read by the Librarian. At first, the Library Mice didn't see C-A-T Cat sneaking around the library.
C-A-T CAT:	(*Sneaks in around the chairs.*)
CHEEZER:	(*Sees the cat.*) L-l-l-look! T-t-t-there's a—
LIBRARIAN MOUSE:	Please, stop interrupting the story, Cheezer.
CHEEZER:	But, there is a c-c-c-cat.
LIBRARIAN MOUSE:	A what?
CHEEZER:	A cat—C-A-T Cat.
LIBRARY MICE:	EEEEEEEEEK!
LIBRARIAN MOUSE:	Where?

CHEEZER:	There! (*Points to cat.*) There is a big, black, furry cat in our library.
C-A-T CAT:	Yes, I am a big, black, furry, *handsome* cat, and I am in your library. I'm searching for fat Library Mice. And, I see plenty around here.
LIBRARY MICE:	EEEEEK! Not me! I'm skinny (*etc. — children add similar lines*).
LIBRARIAN MOUSE:	You are not welcome in our library, Mr. Cat.
C-A-T CAT:	Who cares? I go where I want to go. Before I attack any of you mice, I think I will have a little catnip. (*Takes out a bottle marked "Catnip." He drinks from the bottle, making loud gurgling noises.*) Ha, that was good. (*Wipes his lips with the back of his paw and puts the bottle back in his bag or knapsack. Yawns.*) That catnip makes me sleepy. Before I gobble up any mice, I think I'll have a small cat nap. (*Lays his head on the Librarian's lap and his feet on Cheezer's lap.*)
CHEEZER:	How are we going to get rid of this awful, dangerous sleeping cat?
LIBRARIAN MOUSE:	I haven't a clue, Cheezer. Anyone here have an answer?
LITTLE BITS:	(*Tiny voice.*) We could run away and hide.
LIBRARIAN MOUSE:	That is an excellent idea, Little Bits. We can't lift Cat from our laps, but little Library Mice can run and hide. (*They hide behind chairs.*)
CHEEZER:	We could shoot him, but we don't have a gun. (*Tries to push Cat off his lap.*)
LIBRARIAN MOUSE:	There must be a way to get rid of this heavy cat. (*She tries to free herself.*)
CHEEZER:	But, how? As soon as this fat cat wakes up, we are goners.
C-A-T CAT:	(*Jumps up.*) Right you are, Sonny Boy. This fat cat is now awake. My back hurts. Your laps aren't very comfortable. (*Rubs back.*)
LIBRARIAN MOUSE:	You have been lying on the book I was reading to the Library Mice before you so rudely interrupted us. (*Holds up book.*)
C-A-T CAT:	What's the book about?
CHEEZER:	It's a thriller. It's all about a big, black, furry cat.
C-A-T CAT:	That's my kind of book. Give it to me.

69

CHEEZER:	Don't tear it.
C-A-T- CAT;	(*Takes book.*) I'll do what I please with it. (*Roughly turns some pages.*)
LIBRARIAN MOUSE:	Do you read many books, Mr. C-A-T Cat?
C-A-T CAT:	Naw! Never have time to read books. (*Reads a page.*) Say, this *is* a great book. (*Turns page.*) This is a super book. (*Turns pages.*) This is an awesome book. I'll read it. (*Reads*) That's a fine book.
CHEEZER:	Here, Mr. C-A-T Cat, read this book. I wrote it. You'll like it. (*Gives Cat his book.*)
C-A-T CAT:	(*Reads the book.*)
LITTLE BITS:	Read my book, Mr. Cat, please. (*Gives it to Cat.*)
C-A-T CAT:	Don't mind if I do. (*Reads book.*)
LIBRARY MICE:	(*Rush at Cat.*) Read our books! Read our books! (*They push their books on Cat and knock him to the floor. They jump on Cat.*)
C-A-T CAT:	Mee-ow! I am captured by books and Library Mice. (*Gets up.*) Say, you know what? If you let me up, I'll become a Library Cat.
LITTLE BITS:	You would? And you won't eat us up?
C-A-T CAT:	Naw! I won't eat you up. I really like tuna fish better.
LIBRARIAN MOUSE:	Then you may get a library card and take out as many books as you'd like.
LITTLE BITS:	You can take the books home.
CHEEZER:	But you have to bring them back on time.
LITTLE BITS:	Or you will pay a fine.
C-A-T CAT:	Oh, I will bring all the books back on time.
LIBRARIAN MOUSE:	It is time now for Mice Snacks. Will you join us, Mr. C-A-T Cat?
C-A-T CAT:	I would be delighted. (*Bows*)
CHEEZER:	Remember to eat only the mice snacks.
LITTLE BITS:	And, not me.
LIBRARY MICE:	Not us.
C-A-T CAT:	Never! For I am a good Library Cat.
LIBRARY MICE:	And we are smart Library Mice. (*Exit.*)

The End

Grades 1–4, Long Program: Second Day

Materials Checklist

____ mouse name tags (from previous days)
____ copies of mouse name tag drawing — have a few extra
____ scissors
____ words to "We're Smart Mice" (from this book)
____ crayons or markers
____ "The Bank of Cheese Who-Done-It Caper" story (from this book)
____ mystery books to show
____ straw hat or bandana
____ large cardboard knife
____ rope, yarn or black fabric for mouse tails
____ three pair of dark glasses or funny glasses
____ safety pins (large) or tape
____ mouse ear pattern (from this book)
____ cardboard for mouse ears
____ bandeaus for mouse ears (optional)
____ bobby pins to hold mouse ears
____ black eyebrow pencil
____ red lipstick
____ tissues
____ cold cream
____ mirrors
____ popcorn (popped)
____ lemonade
____ paper napkins
____ paper cups
____ scripts for "Cat Attack"
____ props for "Cat Attack": see page 67. (Not all props are needed for this rehearsal. Some will be made as craft items later in program.)

The Program

Goal

To learn more about mystery and detective stories.

Preparation

Photocopy the drawing of the mouse name tag, page 62—enough copies for each child to have one, plus extra. Photocopy the lyrics for "We're Smart Mice" (page 73)—one copy for each child. Fill small bags with popped corn. Make mouse ear pattern 6" wide by 7½" long per drawing at right and trace onto sturdy cardboard.

Getting Started   (Two groups, 15 minutes)

Hand out mouse name tags from previous day.

Distribute copies of mouse name tag drawing to use for Parents' Day invitations. The children color the drawing and write (librarian can help): "Parents' Day. Place: _____ Date: _____ Time: _____ " (and fill in the appropriate information).

Story Time   (One group, 15 minutes)

The groups join together for Story Time. They sit around the librarian's chair. The librarian reads "The Bank of Cheese Who-Done-It Caper" (pages 75–77.)

Library Time   (One group, 15 minutes)

Talk about mystery stories. Show some mystery story books. Ask: What makes a good mystery story? (Exciting things happen in the story. You don't know who did it until the end. Clues are given, the story keeps you guessing.) What are clues? (Clues are hints along the way of who could have done the dastardly deed. Suspicion should be kept away from the villain, but clues should be there. Make everyone else seem guilty.) Look for clues in other stories.

Have the children tell who their favorite detective is, and why. Name some TV detectives. Ask what their favorite mystery story is. Talk about "The Bank of Cheese Who-Done-It Caper." What are the clues? Who could have robbed the Bank of Cheese?

Sing, "We're Smart Mice" (lyrics below).

Mice Games   (One group, 15 minutes)

"Three Blind Mice." Three children or Library Mice are given dark glasses. Tape fabric, yarn or construction paper tails to their backs. The other Library Mice are the chorus. The librarian is the farmer's wife and wears a straw hat or bandana.

CHORUS (*sings*):	Three blind mice,
	Three blind mice.
LIBRARIAN:	See how they run.
THREE MICE:	(*They run about.*)

"We're Smart Mice"
(To the tune of "Three Blind Mice")

We're smart mice,
We're smart mice,
See how we run,
See how we run,
We didn't run after the farmer's wife,
She would cut off our tails with a carving knife,
We would have made a terrible sight,
We're smart mice.

We're smart mice,
We're smart mice,
See how we run,
See how we run,
We run to take out books at our library,
We are as smart as smart can be
We're smart mice.

CHORUS:	See how they run.
	They all ran after the farmer's wife.
THREE MICE:	(*Run after the farmer's wife.*)
CHORUS:	Who cut off their tails with a carving knife.
LIBRARIAN:	(*Cuts off the mice tails with a big cardboard knife.*)
CHORUS:	Did you ever see such a sight in your life?
THREE MICE:	(*They cry and hold their backsides.*)
CHORUS:	As three blind mice.

The three blind mice give their dark glasses to three other mice, and the game is repeated.

Mice Crafts   (Two groups, 30 minutes)

Mouse Ears and Mouse Make-up. Cut big mouse ears from colored cardboard, using mouse ear pattern. These ears are stapled to a plastic bandeau on an elastic band or they can be bobby-pinned to the hair. Either way, bobby pins are needed.

Mouse tails are made from rope, yarn or black material found in fabric stores. The tails are fastened to the backs of the children with large safety pins or tape.

Mouse make-up consists of black eyebrows, a black nose and black whiskers applied with a black eyebrow pencil. You will need mirrors, tissues and cold cream for taking make-up off. Girls put on red lipstick.

Washup   (One group at a time, 5 minutes)

Snack   (One group, 10 minutes)

Small bags of popcorn, lemonade.

Mice Drama   (One group, 30 minutes)

Rehearse the play "Cat Attack."

Finishing Up   (Two groups, 15 minutes)

Remind the children about Parents' Day. Tell the children to bring a large paper bag for next time for the Mouse Shopping Bags.

Collect name tags.

The Bank of Cheese Who-Done-It Caper

A Detective Story
by
Taffy Jones

Detective Eekers drove by the Bank of Cheese one windy September morning in his sharp cheesemobile. Glancing at the bank clock, Eekers noted it was 11:05 A.M. Suddenly, Detective Eekers slammed on his brakes. He spied Cat coming out of the bank with his paws gripping two money bags.

"Caught you paw-handed," cried Detective Eekers, jumping from his cheesemobile. He poked his rat-gun into the surprised Cat's ribs. Then he looked into the money bags. "There are thousands of dollars in these money bags. Caught you on the spot." Soon old Cat was being hauled off to jail, protesting his innocence. "I didn't rob the Bank of Cheese," cried Cat. "I am innocent."

Detective Eekers drove to his "Get-Em Detective Agency" on Cheddar Street. He had no sooner sat down at his desk when the phone rang. It was Cat, using his one phone call. "Defend me!" he cried. "I am not guilty. I did not rob the Bank of Cheese."

"You were caught with the money bags full of stolen money," replied Detective Eekers.

"That was my hard-earned thousand dollars I drew out of the bank in those money bags. Bank Teller Ellie counted the money out for me. I remember it was Ellie, because she was complaining about her feet hurting. I don't know where the extra money came from. I did not steal any money. All I know is I withdrew one thousand dollars to go on a vacation to Cape Cod. Please, Detective Eekers, take my case. I will pay you well."

"My fee is a hundred dollars a day, plus all the cheese I can eat," replied Detective Eekers.

"You've got it!" shouted Cat, and he hung up the phone.

Detective Eekers scurried to his cheesemobile and headed for the Bank of Cheese. He went in search for clues. Outside the bank he picked up a yellow feather that lay on the ground and stuck it in his detective hat. Then he went inside the bank and checked with Bank Teller Ellie. She confirmed that Cat had withdrawn one thousand dollars that morning, and she also confirmed the bank had been robbed of one hundred and fifty thousand dollars and the money was found in Cats' money bags.

"Were there any suspicious characters hanging around the bank this morning?" asked Detective Eekers.

"Yes, there were, now that you mention it," replied Bank Teller Ellie. "There was Greedy Pig, Slinky Snake and Smelly Skunk."

"I will check out these unsavory guys," said Detective Eekers.

First, Detective Eekers went searching for Slinky Snake. When he found him, he questioned him. "Where were you this morning about eleven o'clock?" asked Detective Eekers, whipping out a small notebook to take notes.

"I was at Bank of Cheese taking out fifty cents from my savings account to buy some bubble gum. Then I slithered over to Fanny Anne's flower garden. I love giving that gal a fright. When she saw me, she jumped and tripped over the garden hose and broke her nose."

"Can you prove it?" asked Detective Eekers.

"Go look at Fanny Anne's nose" replied Slinky Snake as he wiggled away.

Next, Detective Eekers sought out Smelly Skunk. "Were you smelling around the Bank of Cheese this morning?"

"Why the questioning? Why the third degree?" asked Smelly Skunk.

"You were seen raising your tail there," answered Detective Eekers. "The Bank of Cheese was robbed this morning."

Smelly Skunk blinked his small eyes at Detective Eekers. "Now what do you know about that?"

"What do *you* know about that?"

"I know absolutely nothing. I deposited a lot of money this morning from my successful perfume sales. You know my perfume, 'Pass Out,' is a tremendous seller. Then I talked with three of my perfume distributors behind the bank. Check it out with them. Get lost!" Smelly Skunk raised his tail and scurried away.

After much tracking, Detective Eekers found his last suspect. He found Greedy Pig jogging along 109. "Where were you on this windy September morning around eleven o'clock?" asked Detective Eekers, driving his cheesemobile along with the jogging pig.

"I was at my aerobics class," replied Greedy Pig. "We pigs have to keep our figures. I was a smash in my new pink jogging suit. Check it out with the girls. They will tell you where I was."

Detective Eekers had come to a dead-end. He had checked out all the suspects and they had good alibis. The finger pointed at Cat.

76

"Have you found the culprit who robbed the Bank of Cheese at 11:15 A.M.?" asked a bright yellow bird landing on Eekers's shoulder.

"Oh, hello, Jay Bird," replied Detective Eekers. "I have to believe that Cat did it. He was caught with the money bags and the stolen money in them."

Eekers pulled the yellow feather from his hat. "By the way, Jay Bird, where were you when the Bank of Cheese was robbed?"

"I was flying about, minding my own business."

"Did anyone see you flying about?"

"Don't think so. See you. Hope you catch the culprit." Jay Bird flew away.

Suddenly, Detective Eekers knew who had robbed the Bank of Cheese. Do you know who did it?

Was it Slinky Snake?

Was it Smelly Skunk?

Was it Greedy Pig?

Was it Jay Bird?

Why?

Yes, they were all suspects but—

It was Bank Teller Ellie who stole the money. Her feet hurt her so much from all the standing that she wanted to get away from it all. Detective Eekers caught her sneaking out the back door of the bank with a huge purse filled with money.

So Bank Teller Ellie went to jail and Cat was a free cat. Detective Eekers decided he would go to Cape Cod with Cat since Cat would pay all the bills. Cat went for the fish, and Detective Eekers went for the Beach Plum jam.

The End

Grades 1–4, Long Program: Third Day

Materials Checklist

_____ mouse name tags (from previous days)
_____ copies of "Cat Attack Ditty" (from this book)
_____ book about mice for Story Time
_____ film about mice or cats, or a mystery film
_____ large paper bags for Mouse Shopping Bags (children were asked to
      bring, but have some on hand for those who forget)
_____ scissors
_____ white glue
_____ copies of any mouse picture from this book—enough for group
_____ poster paint
_____ markers
_____ stapler
_____ apples
_____ cheese
_____ apple juice
_____ knife for slicing apples and cheese (or slice beforehand)
_____ paper plates
_____ paper napkins
_____ paper cups
_____ scripts for "Cat Attack"
_____ mouse ears
_____ make-up (black eyebrow pencil, red lipstick, blue eyeshadow)
_____ tissues
_____ cold cream
_____ mirrors
_____ props for "Cat Attack": see page 67.

The Program

Goal

Working together with mysteries.

Preparation

Photocopy "The Cat Attack Ditty" (page 80)—one for each child. Photocopy any mouse picture from this book—again, one copy for each. Slice apples (six slices per apple) and cheese.

Getting Started   (Two groups, 15 minutes)

Give out mouse name tags.
Children learn "The Cat Attack Ditty." (Hand out copies of lyrics.)

Story Time   (One group, 15 minutes)

The two groups join together for Story Time. They sit around the librarian's chair. The librarian reads a book about mice or cats. (See Mice and Cats Book List.)

Library Time   (One group, 15 minutes)

Show a film about mice or cats, or a mystery story film.

Mice Games   (One group, 15 minutes)

"Cat and Mouse Game." One child is picked to be "C-A-T Cat" and another to be "Cheezer." Cheezer stands inside the circle and C-A-T Cat tries to get inside the circle and catch Cheezer. The other Library Mice try to help Cheezer. They wave their arms and close in together to keep Cat out of the circle. Meanwhile, Cheezer must go outside of the circle three times. He can dash out anywhere. If he is caught by Cat, then he becomes Cat. If Cheezer makes it out of the circle three times successfully, he picks a new Cheezer, and the game is repeated.

Mice Crafts   (Two groups, 30 minutes)

Mouse Shopping Bags. Each child has a large brown paper bag. Give each child a mouse picture copied from this book. The children color the mice.

Cut off about 2" from the top of the paper bag. This strip will become the handle of the shopping bag. Fold the strip in half and glue the halves together to make the handle stronger. Staple the handle to the shopping bag.

"The Cat Attack Ditty"

Sing to the tune of "Santa Claus Is Coming to Town":

You better watch out,
You better beware.
You better watch out,
You better be scared.
C-A-T Cat is ready to attack.

(Speak loudly with a steady beat:)
Fat Cat! Fat Cat!
Don't Sit on my lap.
Don't attack! Don't attack!
Fat Cat! Fat Cat!

(Speak in regular voices:)
Library Mice, fat cats, and books—
They all go together.
Now things couldn't be better.
There'll be no more cat attacks.
Peace in the library forever.

Glue the mouse to the center of one side of the bag. Write "Mouse Shopping Bag" at top of bag over the mouse. The children write their names at the bottom of the bags.

Washup   (One group at a time, 5 minutes)

Snack   (One group, 10 minutes)

Each child has two slices of apple and two pieces of cheese. (Have extras.) Serve with apple juice.

Mice Drama (One group, 30 minutes)

Dress rehearsal for the play "Cat Attack."

Finishing Up (Two groups, 15 minutes)

Help remove make-up and costumes.

Tell the children to bring a friend to the play. Ask them to tell their parents they may bring cameras and take pictures.

Collect name tags.

Grades 1–4, Long Program: Fourth Day

Materials Checklist

_____ mouse name tags
_____ record or tape for Mice Dancing
_____ record or tape player
_____ Styrofoam small egg for Wee Mouse (each child needs half of egg)
_____ Very small, roly-poly eyes
_____ pipe cleaners for mouse tail for Wee Mouse (each child needs half a pipe cleaner)
_____ crewel needle threaded with monofilament line, or paint brush, broom bristles or thin, stiff wire
_____ acrylic paints
_____ paintbrushes
_____ Styrofoam painted yellow for "cheese," or half a yellow sponge for each piece of "cheese"
_____ scissors
_____ Sobo glue (special glue that works on Styrofoam)
_____ cupcakes with mouse faces
_____ paper napkins
_____ paper cups
_____ soft drinks
_____ scripts for play "Cat Attack" (if not memorized)
_____ words to "We're Smart Mice" and "The Cat Attack Ditty" (if not memorized)
_____ props for play "Cat Attack": see page 67.
_____ mouse ears
_____ make-up (black eyebrow pencil, red lipstick, blue eyeshadow)
_____ tissues
_____ cold cream
_____ mirrors
_____ chairs for audience

The Program

Goal

To present a mystery play for audience.

Preparation

If Styrofoam is to be used for Wee Mouse's "cheese," paint yellow and let dry. Make or purchase cupcakes and decorate with mouse faces: chocolate chips for eyes and nose, red cinnamon candies for a mouth, toothpicks for whiskers (two on each side). Set up chairs for Parents' Day audience.

Getting Started   (Two groups, 15 minutes)

Give out mouse name tags.
Go over "The Cat Attack Ditty."

Story Time   (One group, 15 minutes)

Read a book about mice or cats. (See Mice and Cats Book List.)

Library Time

No library time on play day.

Mice Games   (One group, 15 minutes)

"Mice Dancing." Play a popular or lively tape or record. The Library Mice dance to this music. When the music stops (suddenly), the Library Mice hold a mouse pose, or become a mouse statue. Start the music again and repeat as many times as desired.

One child is chosen to be C-A-T Cat. When the music stops, the Library Mouse who Cat touches is out. Start the music again and Cat paws out another mouse. This is repeated until there is only one mouse on the dance floor. This Library Mouse is the winner and gets some cheese, or this Library Mouse is chosen to be C-A-T Cat to play the game again.

Mice Crafts   (Two groups, 30 minutes)

Make a Wee Mouse on a piece of cheese. Show the Wee Mouse (next page). Cut a small foam egg (2" size) in half. Each child receives half an egg, which he or she paints any color with acrylic paint. This becomes the body of the Wee Mouse.

A 2" × 3" styrofoam painted with yellow acrylic paint is a piece of cheese for the Wee Mouse to sit on, or use half a yellow sponge to be the cheese.

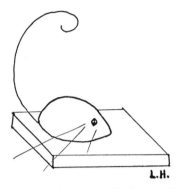

L.H.

Wee mouse

Each child has half a pipe cleaner (color optional) for the mouse's tail. Glue two tiny roly-poly eyes. Thread crewel needle with monofilament line and pull through the nose area for the whiskers. Paint brush bristles or thin stiff wire or broom bristles make good whiskers.

(Use Sobo glue. Not all glues will work on styrofoam. Some glues make the styrofoam melt away.)

Washup (One group at a time, 10 minutes)

Snack (One group, 10 minutes)

Cupcakes with mouse faces, soft drink.

Mice drama (One group, 45 minutes)

Present "Cat Attack."

Finishing Up (Two groups, 15 minutes)

Have parents take pictures while the children are still in costume. Take off make-up.

Tell the children what great Library Mice they have been. Tell them to visit the library often and take out mystery and detective stories to read. Tell the children to try writing a mystery story at home and read it to someone.

Children take home name tags, crafts, mouse ears, etc.

Library Mice:
Grades 1–4, Short Program
Time: 2 days; 1 1/2 hours each day

Getting Started: Mouse name tags (10 min.)
Story Time: "The Bank of Cheese Who-Done-It Caper" (10 min.)
Library Time: Talk about mystery stories;
Sleuthing Out the Card Catalog (10 min.)
Mice Games: "Find the Mouse Ears" (5 min.)
Mice Crafts: Mouse Sneakers (15 min.)
Washup and Snack: Peanut butter crackers, fruit punch (15 min.)
Mice Drama: "The Bank of Cheese Who-Done-It Caper"—
read through and practice (15 min.)
Finishing Up (5 min.)

SECOND DAY
Getting Started: Big Mice Ears and Mice Tails (10 min.)
Story Time: Book about mice or cats (10 min.)
Library Time: Sleuth out mice and cat books (10 min.)
Mice Games: Mouse Dancing (5 min.)
Mice Crafts: Mouse Bookmarks (15 min.)
Washup and Snack: Mouse cookies, chocolate milk (15 min.)
Mice Drama: Present "The Bank of Cheese Who-Done-It Caper" (20 min.)
Finishing Up (5 min.)

Grades 1–4, Short Program: First Day

Materials Checklist

____ mouse name tags (from this book)—have a few extra
____ "The Bank of Cheese Who-Done-It Caper" play and story (from this book)
____ markers or crayons
____ yarn for mouse name tags
____ white cardboard backing for mouse name tags (optional)
____ scissors
____ book for Story Time
____ mystery story books
____ small cardboard or construction paper mouse ears
____ pom poms or craft cotton balls for mice sneakers (color optional)
____ pipe cleaners
____ small roly-poly eyes
____ white glue
____ monofilament line or black yarn
____ paper napkins
____ paper cups
____ peanut butter
____ crackers
____ fruit juice
____ knife to spread peanut butter

The Program

Goal

To sharpen a child's observation and imagination.

Preparation

Photocopy the mouse name tag on page 62—each child will need one. You may wish to further prepare name tags for Grades 1–2 (see "Getting Started" on page 87). Cut several "mouse ears" out of construction paper or cardboard and hide them around the library for Mice Games. Photocopy scripts for the play "The Bank of Cheese Who-Done-It Caper" (pages 75–77) and "Sleuthing Out the Card Catalog" (page 43)—enough for group.

Getting Started   (Two groups*, 10 minutes)

The mice are in two groups or mouse circles at opposite ends of the room. Give out mouse name tags. The children write their names on the name tags (or the librarian can do it ahead of time) and color them.

Story Time   (One group, 10 minutes)

The children sit around the librarian, who reads them the story "The Bank of Cheese Who-Done-It Caper" (pages 75–77 of this book).

Library Time   (One group, 10 minutes)

Talk about mystery stories.
Using the photocopied sheets for "Sleuthing Out the Card Catalog," find mystery stories in the catalog and in the stacks.

Mice Games   (One group, 5 minutes)

"Find the Mouse Ears." The children are told about the hidden ears (see "Preparation") and asked to see how many they can find. The child who finds the most ears is the winner. If time, talk about clues in a mystery book.

Mice Crafts   (Two groups, 15 minutes)

Show children the drawing of the Mouse Sneaker (page 88). Give each child one craft cotton ball (any color), one pipe cleaner (any color), two craft (roly-poly) eyes, and monofilament whiskers for their sneaker mouse. (Black yarn can also be used for whiskers.) Pinch the face of the craft cotton ball together and glue on the eyes. Shape a pipe cleaner for the tail and bring it under the sneaker mouse's body. Glue it securely and pull down a tiny loop for the sneaker strings (or bracelet) to go through. These are fun mice and every Library Mouse would like one.

*"Two groups" signifies that division of a large group is appropriate or desirable. You may prefer not to divide small groups.

Mouse Sneakers (or bracelets, lower right).

88

Washup   (One group at a time, 5 minutes)

Snack   (One group, 10 minutes)

Peanut butter on crackers, fruit punch.

Mice Drama   (One group, 20 minutes)

Read through the play "The Bank of Cheese Who-Done-It Caper."
Choose the parts.
Do the play with the characters.
Talk about the costumes, make-up and props.

Finishing Up   (Two groups, 5 minutes)

Explain that the next day will be Parents' Day, when parents and friends can come to see the play.

Collect mouse name tags.

Grades 1–4, Short Program: Second Day

Materials Checklist

____ mouse name tags (from previous day)
____ mouse ear pattern (from this book)
____ cardboard for mouse ears
____ bobby pins or plastic headbands
____ book for Story Time
____ record or tape for mouse dancing
____ record or tape player
____ mouse bookmarks (from this book)
____ scissors
____ white glue
____ markers or crayons
____ construction paper, braided yarn, or craft fur for mouse tails
____ mouse cookies
____ chocolate milk
____ paper napkins
____ paper cups
____ costumes and props for "The Bank of Cheese Who-Done-It Caper"
       Play (see page 94)
____ chairs for audience
____ make-up (black eyebrow pencil, lipstick, blue eye shadow)
____ cleansing cream
____ tissues
____ mirrors
____ safety pins

The Program

Goal

To find that a good mystery story is as good as a mystery story on TV.

Mouse face for mouse bookmark (previous page).

Preparation

Follow directions for mouse ear pattern (page 72) and trace onto sturdy cardboard. Photocopy Mouse Bookmark (page 91)—enough for each child to have one, plus a few extra. Also photocopy mouse face (part of mouse bookmark), this page. Set up chairs for audience. You may wish to bake cookies for snack (though store-bought will do).

Getting Started (Two groups, 10 minutes)

(Unless a large number of children.) Give out mouse name tags. Make mouse ears and do mouse make-up.

Story Time (One group, 10 minutes)

The children sit around the librarian, who reads them a book about mice or cats.

Library Time (One group, 10 minutes)

The children sleuth out as many cat and mouse books as they can find. Then they sit around in a circle and show their books and give the titles.

Mice Games   (One group, 5 minutes)

Mice Dancing. Put on a tape or record of lively (or Mousy!) music. The Library Mice dance. Stop the music suddenly. The children hold a mouse position, make mouse faces, and say "EEEEEEK!" Music starts again. Repeat stopping and posing. Then the children form a circle and dance around the circle like mice. At the end the children take turns to see who can say "EEEEEEK" the loudest, the softest, the funniest, the most mouse-like, etc.

Mice Crafts   (One group, 15 minutes)

Mice Bookmarks. The children color the mouse and cup and cut out. Then they color and cut out the mouse's face, and paste the mouse face on the *back* of attached face. When it is closed, you should see the mouse's face, and when it is open, you see the word "Read."

Washup   (One group at a time, 5 minutes)

Snack   (One group, 10 minutes)

"Mouse Cookies" (any cookies) and chocolate milk.

Mice Drama   (One group, 20 minutes)

Present "The Bank of Cheese Who-Done-It Caper" play (pages 94–99).

Finishing Up   (Two groups, 5 minutes)

Take pictures, take off make-up. Children take home mouse name tags, crafts, etc.

Tell the children they have been good Library Mice, and ask them to come again.

The Bank of Cheese Who-Done-It Caper

A Play
by
Taffy Jones

Characters:

ANNOUNCER
DETECTIVE EEKERS
CAT
GREEDY PIG
SLINKY SNAKE
SMELLY SKUNK
JAY BIRD
SECURITY GUARD RATSON

Note: Characters can be either sex.

Props and Costumes:

DETECTIVE EEKERS:	Raincoat, detective hat, spy glass, small notebook and pencil, yellow feather, glasses (optional)
CAT:	Black, furry cat hood with ears, a tail, furry paws. (Cat suit is optional.) Whiskers and heavy eyebrows (black eyebrow pencil), two money bags (paper or canvas bags with large dollar signs on them).
GREEDY PIG:	Flashy jogging suit, sweat headband, pig nose (optional) and curly tail.
SLINKY SNAKE:	Green hood, green shirt or blouse and pin or paint spots on it. Paint slanty eyes with make-up.
SMELLY SKUNK:	Black pants or skirt, white top, long black and white furry tail, large perfume bottle with "Pass Out" on it.
JAY BIRD:	Yellow shirt, white pants, red or orange socks, yellow cardboard beak with elastic to hold in place. Yellow feathers, safety pins, red lipstick and blue eyeshadow.

SECURITY GUARD: Blue suit, police badge, police hat, gun and holster, boots, dark glasses, mustache (optional).
Also need "The Bank of Cheese" with a large clock.

The Play:

ANNOUNCER: The play takes place in front of The Bank of Cheese on a windy September morning. Detective Eekers drives by the bank in his [her] sharp cheesemobile, just as Cat comes leaping down the steps of the bank with two money bags in his [her] paws. Detective Eekers jumps out of the cheesemobile and surprises Cat (*running in with two money bags*).

EEKERS: Hold it, Cat! Caught you with your paws on the money bags. (*He grabs Cat.*)

CAT: The money in these bags is mine. (*He holds up bags.*)

EEKERS: A likely story. You're a Cat burglar with a record.

CAT: I tell you, Detective Eekers, the money in these two money bags is mine.

EEKERS: I will check out your story. How much money do you have in those bags?

CAT: I had Bank Teller Ellie put five hundred dollars in this bag (*pats the right bag*), and five hundred dollars in this bag (*pats the other bag*).

EEKERS: (*Looks in the money bags.*) There's more than five thousand dollars in these two money bags. I can tell without counting.

CAT: How can that be? There should be only *one* thousand dollars in the bags—five hundred in each bag.

EEKERS: Off to jail you go. I will find Security Guard Ratson.

CAT: (*Meows loudly.*)

EEKERS: Stop the meowing, Cat. (*Starts to exit with Cat.*)

CAT: (*Pulls back.*) Hold on, Detective Eekers, I didn't rob the Bank of Cheese. You are the greatest detective since Ratbo. Take my case. Prove I am innocent.

EEKERS: But I think you are guilty.

CAT: But I'm not guilty. I can pay you well (*Holds up the money bags.*) I took the thousand out for a vacation at Cape Cod.

EEKERS: Well—

95

CAT:	(*Shakes the money bags.*) Think of the money, Eekers. Think of justice.
EEKERS:	I am—all right. You say you are innocent. Then that means someone else did it. Someone else must have slipped the stolen bank money into your money bags, at the time you were at the Bank Teller's window.
CAT:	Sounds good, Eekers. That's great detecting. They don't call you famous for nothing.
EEKERS:	Who else was near the Bank Teller's window when you were withdrawing your money?
CAT:	Let me see. There was a line behind me. Oh, I remember, there was Slinky Snake.
EEKERS:	A very slippery customer.
CAT:	And, Greedy Pig—
EEKERS:	Greedy Pig is always out to get all he can get.
CAT:	Smelly Skunk was there, too.
EEKERS:	Smelly Skunk? Three unsavory characters. Anyone else near Bank Teller Ellie?
CAT:	Nope.
EEKERS:	I will check out these suspects. (*Sees a yellow feather on the ground. Picks it up and puts it in his detective hat.*)
CAT:	Speaking of the suspects, here come the nasties now.
PIG, SKUNK AND SNAKE:	(*Enter with a character animal walk and speak like the animal.*)
EEKERS:	You three are just who I want to talk to about the Bank of Cheese robbery.
PIG:	We know our rights, oink, oink. We don't have to talk to you if we don't want to.
SNAKE & SKUNK:	Tell him, Greedy. Tell him.
EEKERS:	Better to talk now than in court.
SNAKE:	What do you want to know? (*Wiggles.*)
EEKERS:	Slinky Snake, where were you around eleven o'clock this morning? (*Takes out small notebook and pencil.*)
SNAKE:	I withdrew fifty cents from the Bank of Cheese this morning to buy some bubble gum. Then I slithered over to Fanny Anne's house and wriggled around in her flower garden. I did a

scare job on Fanny Anne. She jumped and tripped over the garden hose and broke her nose. Check it out.

EEKERS: (*Writes in notebook.*) Trips and breaks her nose. Greedy Pig, where were you this morning around eleven o'clock? (*Starts to write in his notebook.*)

PIG: I put my week's earnings in the bank and curly-tailed it to my aerobics class. My jogging suit was such a hit, everyone noticed me. Oink, oink. Everyone will tell you I was there. (*Exits.*)

EEKERS: Now, for you, Smelly Skunk. You are the last of my suspects for this Bank Caper.

SKUNK: I cashed a lot of checks this morning at the Bank of Cheese. I am a millionaire from my new perfume, "Pass Out." Later, I talked with two of my perfume distributors behind the bank. They will vouch for me.

CAT: Oh, sure. Of course, they will. All you guys stick together.

SKUNK: That's no fur off my back. I am clean. (*Exits.*)

EEKERS: I am sorry, Cat, but nothing checks out. You were the one caught coming out of the Bank of Cheese with two money bags full of hot cash.

CAT: But I didn't steal it.

EEKERS: So you say, but the evidence points your way.

JAY BIRD: (*Enters.*) Hello, Eekers. (*Flaps arms.*) Had any good detective cases lately?

EEKERS: Oh, hello, Jay Bird. I am on one now. I call it, "The Bank of Cheese Who-Done-It Caper."

JAY BIRD: Who did done it?

EEKERS: You mean, who did did it?

JAY BIRD: No, I mean, who done it? (*Shakes a feather loose.*)

EEKERS: I don't have a clue who done it. (*Picks up the feather. Looks in his notebook.*) Wait a minute, where were you, Jay Bird, at eleven o'clock today?

JAY BIRD: At five minutes after eleven? I was nowhere near the Bank of Cheese, I can tell you that.

EEKERS: Where were you?

JAY BIRD: I was flying over Moultonboro, which is ten miles from here.

EEKERS:	At exactly five minutes after eleven, I drove my cheesemobile by the Bank of Cheese, which had just been robbed. Jay Bird, you being a well-known jailbird, I think *you* robbed the Bank of Cheese and slipped the money into Cat's money bags. You made a quick get-away, planning to pick up the money later when Cat wasn't home.
JAY BIRD:	You can't prove it.
EEKERS:	Oh, yes, I can.
ANNOUNCER:	How did Detective Eekers solve the Bank of Cheese Who-Done-It Caper? Can anyone tell me who done—I mean who did it? (*The children give answers to the questions and reasons.*) All right. Here is the answer. We go back to Detective Eekers.
EEKERS:	I know, without a doubt, that you, Jay Bird, robbed the Bank of Cheese this morning at 11:05 A.M. You, Jay Bird, not only knew the exact time of the robbery, but you left one big clue. This yellow feather of yours matches the yellow feather left at the scene of the crime. (*Pulls the yellow feather from his hat.*) You left this yellow feather at the time the bank was robbed. If you dropped it before 11:05 A.M., it would have been blown away by the wind. It's a windy day today. You lost your feather at exactly 11:05 A.M., the time the bank was robbed, and I found it. I looked at the bank clock, so I know the exact time of the robbery.
JAY BIRD:	(*Looks at feather.*) Come on, Detective Eekers, that's not *my* feather.
EEKERS:	Once we check out this feather, and it will check out that it *is* yours, it will prove *you* robbed the Bank of Cheese, and not Cat.
JAY BIRD:	O.K. Eekers. I did the job. You caught me with one feather down.
EEKERS:	Here comes Security Guard Ratson.
RATSON:	(*Enters.*)
EEKERS:	Haul this jailbird to the cage. She robbed the Bank of Cheese this morning.
RATSON:	Come on, Jay Bird, your bird is cooked. (*Takes Jay Bird Away.*)

CAT: Thanks, Detective Eekers. You did it again. You made me a free cat. I will be off to Cape Cod for vacation after all.

EEKERS: Say Cat. I am going with you. I love Cape Cod. I need a vacation. Remember, you owe me a bundle. You can go for the fish, and I will go for the Beach Plum jam.

The End

Library Mice:
Preschool–Kindergarten, Long Program
Time: 2 days; 1 1/2 hours each day

Getting Started: Color Mouse name tags (10 min.)
Story Time: Book about mice or cats (10 min.)
Library Time: Library talk, short library tour (10 min.)
Mice Games: "Finger Printing" (5 min.)
Mice Crafts: Big Cat Faces (15 min.)
Washup and Snack: Cookies and milk (15 min.)
Mice Drama: "A Small Bank of Cheese Who-Done-It Caper"—
read-through and practice (20 min.)
Finishing Up (5 min.)

SECOND DAY
Getting Started: Cheesemobiles (10 min.)
Story Time: "The Bank of Cheese Who-Done-It-Caper" (story) (10 min.)
Library Time: Finding mystery, mice and cat books (10 min.)
Mice Games: "Hide the Cheesemobile" (5 min.)
Mice Crafts: Mice and Cat Paper Dolls (15 min.)
Washup and Snack: Cheese crackers or cheese balls and fruit punch (15 min.)
Mice Drama: Present "A Small Bank of Cheese Who-Done-It Caper" (20 min.)
Finishing Up (5 min.)

Preschool–Kindergarten Long Program:
First Day

Materials Checklist

_____ mouse name tags (from this book)—have a few extra
_____ yarn for mouse name tags and for Big Cat Faces
_____ paper punch
_____ white cardboard for name tag backing and for Big Cat Faces (optional)
_____ scissors
_____ white glue
_____ crayons or markers
_____ book selections for each child
_____ mouse ear pattern
_____ tongue depressors, popsicle sticks or straws for stickpuppets
_____ two books about mice or cats
_____ black ink pad
_____ white paper in 4 × 4 sheets (or your choice of size)
_____ paper towels
_____ Big Cat Face (from this book)—each child receives one
_____ colored cardboard for mouse ears
_____ cookies
_____ milk
_____ paper napkins
_____ paper cups

The Program

Goals:

To have fun with mystery stories and to work together in a play.

Preparation

Photocopy the mouse name tag on pages 62–63 (you may wish to enlarge it)—enough for group plus a few extra. For this age group it is best to
do most of the work on name tags ahead of time—cut them out, add cardboard backing if you like, punch holes in top and thread yarn through. Also

Big Cat Face (enlarge to 5½ inches wide, or use as is)

photocopy the Big Cat Face on page 102, enough for group plus extra. (Enlarge by hand or on copier.)

Getting Started   (Two groups,* 10 minutes)

The children are in their mouse circles. Give each child a mouse name tag. Children color the name tags and write their names on them.

Story Time   (One group, 10 minutes)

The children sit around the librarian in a mouse circle. The librarian reads them a book about mice or cats.

Library Time   (One group, 10 minutes)

Talk about things in the library. Give clues for things you see in the library. *Example:* I see something that is big, made of wood, and holds many bright things made of paper. What is it? What were the clues given?

Take a short tour of the library. If a large number of children, take two groups, and have an assistant read a detective book to one group as the other is touring.

Mice Games   (One group, 5 minutes)

"Finger Printing." Have sheets of white paper about 4"x4" for each child. Have the children line up in front of a table to be fingerprinted. Roll each child's index finger on the black ink pad. After all the children have been fingerprinted (have paper towels on hand for wiping fingers!) they draw mouse ears on their finger prints. They add a mouse tail, eyes, nose and whiskers to the finger print to make a mouse picture. They sign their names to the finger print mouse drawings.

Mice Crafts   (Two groups, 15 minutes)

Big Cat Faces. Cut out the Big Cat Face.

Draw the outline of Big Cat on a piece of white cardboard.

Glue the Big Cat drawing to the cut-out white cardboard. (Using the cardboard backing is optional.)

---

*"Two groups" notation signifies that division of a large group is appropriate or desirable for an activity. You may prefer not to divide small groups.

Punch four holes in Big Cat's ears for the yarn or string to go through. Big Cat then hangs on your neck.

Washup   (One group at a time, 5 minutes)

Snack   (One group, 10 minutes)

Serve Toll House cookies or any favorite cookies and milk. Cats love milk!

Mice Drama   (One group, 20 minutes)

Read "A Small Bank of Cheese Who-Done-It Caper" play (pages 94–99). Choose the characters. Go through the play with the characters acting out their parts as the librarian reads.

Finishing Up   (Two groups, 5 minutes)

Explain that the next day will be Parents' Day, when parents and friends can come see the play.

Collect name tags.

Preschool–Kindergarten Long Program:
Second Day

Materials Checklist

____ mouse name tags (from previous day)
____ crayons and markers
____ scissors
____ book for Story Time
____ yellow sponges for cheesemobiles
____ mouse paper dolls (from this book)
____ white cardboard for backing (optional)
____ cheese balls or cheese crackers
____ fruit juice
____ paper napkins
____ paper cups
____ make-up and costumes for play (see pages 94, 95)
____ cleansing cream
____ tissues
____ chairs for Parents' Day audience

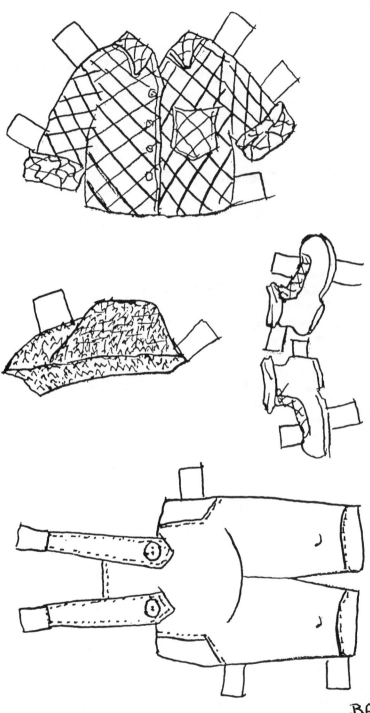

BA

106

Mouse paper doll. Clothes opposite.

The Program

Preparation

Copy the paper dolls and clothes, pages 106–107. Set up chairs for Parents' Day audience.

Getting Started   (Two groups, 10 minutes)

The children are in mouse circles.

Give out mouse name tags and have the children color them. As they work the librarian cuts a cheesemobile from a yellow sponge. This will be used in the "Hide the Cheesemobile" game.

Story Time   (One group, 10 minutes)

Read the *story* "The Bank of Cheese Who-Done-It Caper" (pages 75–77). Ask: How is this different from the play? How is a play different from a story? (Characters say the lines. The action is in front of you in a play.)

Library Time   (One group, 10 minutes)

With the librarian's help, the children find mystery books and books about mice and cats. The children go back to their mouse circles and each one shows his or her book.

Mice Games   (One group, 5 minutes)

"Find the Cheesemobile." The Library Mice cover their eyes with their hands. The librarian hides the sponge cheesemobile made during "Getting Started." The children search for the cheesemobile. Tell the children the boundaries of where the cheesemobile is hidden. The child who finds the cheesemobile gets to hide it, and the game is repeated.

Mice Crafts   (Two groups, 15 minutes)

Mice Paper Dolls. Each child receives a mouse paper doll to color. Then they cut out the paper doll and clothes.

Remember, do not cut the tabs on the clothes. A cardboard backing can be added to the paper dolls for more durability (optional).

Washup   (One group at a time, 5 minutes)

Snack   (One group, 10 minutes)

Serve cheese crackers or cheese balls and fruit juice.

Mice Drama   (One group, 20 minutes)

Present "A Small Bank of Cheese Caper" *(play).*

For make-up, use black eyebrow pencil for noses and whiskers. Mouse and cat ears and tails, etc., are optional.

Finishing Up   (Two groups, 5 minutes)

Some children will want to remove their make-up. Have cleansing cream and tissues handy.

Tell the children what great Library Mice they have been. Tell them it's O.K. to come often to the library. Tell them to watch TV, but read good books, too. Remind them they can take out mystery and detective books from the library. Tell them to also look for other kinds of books.

The children take home name tags, crafts, etc.

Library Mice:
Preschool–Kindergarten, Short Program
Time: 2 days; 1 1/2 hours each day

Getting Started: Mouse name tags (10 min.)
Story Time: "The Bank of Cheese Who-Done-It Caper" story (10 min.)
Library Time: Library Talk, detective work (10 min.)
Mice Games: Pin the Nose on the Mouse (5 min.)
Mice Crafts: Mice Paper Dolls (15 min.)
Washup and Snack: Cake made like a mouse or cat, Kool-aid (15 min.)
Mice Drama: "A Small Bank of Cheese Who-Done-It Caper" (20 min.)
Finishing Up (5 min.)

Materials Checklist

____ mouse name tags (from this book)–have a few extra
____ yarn for mouse name tags
____ paper punch
____ white cardboard for name tag backing and for paper doll backing (optional)
____ enlarge mouse stickpuppet drawing
____ scissors
____ white glue
____ crayons and markers
____ black paper mouse nose
____ thumb tacks and long straight pins
____ blindfold
____ "'The Bank of Cheese Who-Done-It Caper" *story* (from this book)
____ mice paper dolls and clothes
____ cake
____ Kool-aid
____ paper cups
____ paper napkins
____ plastic forks (optional)
____ script for play "A Small Bank of Cheese Who-Done-It Caper" (from this book)
____ black eyebrow pencil, animal ears and tails (optional)
____ cleansing cream
____ tissues
____ chairs for audience

The Program

Goals

To acquaint the younger child with the library; to have a child discover good books; to have younger children to work together for a common goal; and to improve motor and thinking skills.

Preparation

Photocopy the mouse name tag (page 62) and the mice paper dolls and clothes (pages 106–107), making enough copies for each child to have one of everything. Enlarge the mouse drawing (page 62) to as large a size as possible. Make a large black paper mouse nose. Tell the parents they may come for the play reading, if it is decided to have parent participation. Make a cake shaped like a cat or mouse, or use any store-bought cake.

Getting Started (Two groups,* 10 minutes)

The children sit in mouse circles (tables or on the floor). They color their mice name tags and write their names on them. Then they can name their name tag mice.

Story Time (One group, 10 minutes)

Read "The Bank of Cheese Who-Done-It Caper" *story* (pages 75–77). Talk about being a detective.

Library Time (One group, 10 minutes)

Go to the book stacks and find some detective stories. Talk about the books. Do a little detective work: See who can find first the card catalog, a pencil, a stuffed toy, water fountain, books on cats, a new book arrival, etc.

*"Two group" notation signifies that division of large group is appropriate or desirable. You may prefer not to divide smaller groups.

Mice Games   (One group, 5 minutes)

"Pin the Nose on the Mouse." Blindfold the children one at a time and place a nose with a pin in it in their hand; turn them around and head them toward the large mouse that has been taped to the wall. Each child has a turn to pin on the nose. The child who pins it closest to the nose is the winner.

Mice Crafts   (Two groups, 15 minutes)

The children color the paper doll and clothes. Then, they cut out the paper doll and clothes. Some may need a little help with the cutting. Remember, do not cut the tabs on the clothes.

Washup   (One group at a time, 5 minutes)

Snack   (One group, 10 minutes)

Cake and Kool-aid

Mice Drama   (One group, 20 minutes)

Read the *play* "A Small Bank of Cheese Who-Done-It-Caper" (pages 113–116).

Choose the characters.

Read the play again with the characters acting out their parts. The parents may be asked to attend.

Finishing Up   (One group, 5 minutes)

Tell the children what good little Library Mice they have been, and to come to the library again.

Tell the children to have fun and learn a lot by reading good books, just as they do by watching television.

Take home mouse name tags, crafts, etc.

A Small Bank of Cheese Who-Done-It Caper

(A Small Play for Preschool and Kindergarten)
by
Taffy Jones

Characters:

DETECTIVE EEKERS
CAT
SLINKY SNAKE
SMELLY SKUNK
GREEDY PIG
JAY BIRD

Note: Characters may be either sex.

The children wear ears, tails, noses, appropriate to their character. This is optional, if costumes are not possible, or thought not needed for this simple play.

The librarian reads the play as the children act out the parts, except where the characters speak for themselves.

LIBRARIAN:	The play takes place in front of the Bank of Cheese on a September morning. Detective Eekers has just caught Cat coming out of the Bank of Cheese with money bags in his [her] hand.
CAT:	(*Runs in with a money bag in his or her paw.*)
EEKERS:	(*Runs after Cat.*) Got ya!
LIBRARIAN:	Detective Eekers caught Cat paw-handed coming out of the Bank of Cheese with stolen money in his money bags. "It's off to jail for you, you old cat burglar." Detective Eekers grabbed Cat and started to haul him off to jail.

113

Library Mice

EEKERS:	(*Grabs Cat and starts to move away.*)
LIBRARIAN:	"I did not steal any money from the Bank of Cheese", cried Cat. "The money in these money bags is mine. I just took it out of the bank to go on a vacation. I don't know where the extra money came from."
CAT:	(*Holds up money bags and shakes his head.*)
LIBRARIAN:	"How much is in the money bags? asked Detective Eekers. "One thousand dollars", replied Cat.
EEKERS:	(*Looks into the first money bag.*)
LIBRARIAN:	"There's thousands of dollars, at least, in this bag."
EEKERS:	(*Looks in other bag.*)
LIBRARIAN:	"And there's thousands in here. Come on, you cat burglar, off to jail with you."
CAT:	(*Kneels and pleads.*)
LIBRARIAN:	"But, I am innocent. You are a great detective. Find out who did it. I will pay you well."
CAT:	(*Stands and raises money bag.*)
LIBRARIAN:	"All right, to see justice done, I will defend you," replied Detective Eekers. "I hope it proves out that you are not guilty." "It will," replied cat. "Who else was at the scene of the crime at the time the Bank of Cheese was robbed?" asked Detective Eekers, picking up a yellow feather and putting it in his [her] detective's hat.
EEKERS:	(*Picks up a yellow feather and puts it in his hat. Color of feather is optional.*)
LIBRARIAN:	"Let me see," replied Cat. "Slinky Snake, Smelly Skunk and Greedy Pig were hanging around the bank when I was there. Look—"
CAT:	(*Points.*)
LIBRARIAN:	"Here comes the suspects now."
PIG, SNAKE, SKUNK:	(*Enter and stand in a straight line facing the audience.*)
PIG:	I am Greedy Pig.
SNAKE:	I am Slinky Snake.
SKUNK:	I am Smelly Skunk.
CAT:	I am Cat.
EEKERS:	I know that. (*Takes out a small notebook from his pocket and writes in it.*)

LIBRARIAN:	"Where were you unsavory characters this morning around 11:00 A.M.?" asked Detective Eekers.
	"I was at my aerobics class", replied Greedy Pig. "We pigs have to watch our figures, you know. Check it out."
PIG:	(*Jogs up and down.*)
LIBRARIAN:	Then Detective Eekers turned to Slinky Snake. "Where were you this A.M. around eleven o'clock?"
	"I was slithering around in Fanny Anne's flower garden," replied Slinky Snake. "I scared her so badly, she tripped over the garden hose and broke her nose. Check it out."
SNAKE:	(*Wiggles all over the place.*)
LIBRARIAN:	"O.K. Smelly, what about you?"
	"I was sniffing out my new perfume called 'Pass Out.' I was with two of my distributors," answered Smelly Skunk. "Check it out."
SKUNK:	(*Walks towards Detective Eekers. Eekers holds his nose.*)
JAY BIRD:	(*Flies in—a very fast talker.*) Hello, hello. What's up?
LIBRARIAN:	"Oh, hello, Jay Bird. Somebody robbed the Bank of Cheese around eleven this morning," replied Detective Eekers.
	"So, the great Detective Eekers is on a sleuthing job?" Jay Bird ruffled his [her] feathers and a feather flew out.
JAY BIRD:	(*Lets a feather fall out of his [her] hand—feather has been concealed in his [her] hand.*) Who done it? Who done it?
LIBRARIAN:	Detective Eekers took off his detective hat, scratched his head, and then put his hat back on and said, "I think I know who did it."
	Was it Greedy Pig who robbed the Bank of Cheese?
PIG:	NO! NO! NO! NO!
LIBRARIAN:	Was it Slinky Snake who robbed the Bank of Cheese)
SNAKE:	NO! NO! NO! NO!
LIBRARIAN:	Did Cat do it?

CAT:	I most positively, absolutely did *not* rob the Bank of Cheese.
LIBRARIAN:	Then, who did? Can any of you children in the audience guess who robbed the Bank of Cheese this morning?
AUDIENCE:	(*Children participation. They say who they think robbed the Bank of Cheese.*)
LIBRARIAN:	I will tell you who did the crime. *Jay Bird* robbed the Bank of Cheese. Do you know how Detective Eekers knew this?
AUDIENCE:	(*Children participation.*)
LIBRARIAN:	Right. Jay Bird's feather was found at the scene of the crime. Detective Eekers showed Jay Bird the feather from his hat and how it matched the feather on the ground from Jay Bird himself [herself].
EEKERS:	(*Takes the feather from his hat and matches it with the feather that has fallen on the ground.*)
LIBRARIAN:	Jay Bird confessed to stealing the money from the Bank of Cheese. Cat was free to go on his vacation with his *one* thousand dollars.
EEKERS:	(*Shakes hands with Cat.*)
LIBRARIAN:	Jay Bird went to jail.
PIG, SNAKE, SKUNK:	(*Take Jay Bird off to jail.*)
JAY BIRD:	It's the bird cage for me. (*Exits.*)
LIBRARIAN:	Cat takes Detective Eekers on vacation with him. They go to Cape Cod. Cat went for the fish, and Detective Eekers went for the Beach Plum jam.
EEKERS & CAT:	(*Exit arm in arm.*)

The End

3. Library Dinosaurs

An archaeology theme in the Library Dinosaurs programs will encourage children to "dig deep" into books. They will learn that there are often many different books about one subject, and talk about library cards for checking them out. As in the other programs, the children will learn to work together in performing songs and producing plays (some will even make their own stage).

Library Dinosaurs:
Grades 1–4, Long Program
Time: 4 days; 2 1/2 hours each day

FIRST DAY
Getting Started: Dinosaur name tags and roll call (15 min.)
Story Time: Book about dinosaurs (15 min.)
Library Time: Library talk, library tour (15 min.)
Dinosaur Games: "Drop the Dinosaur Bone" (15 min.)
Dinosaur Crafts: Dinosaur Hats (30 min.)
Washup and Snack: Dinosaur cookies, fruit punch (15 min.)
Dinosaur Drama: "Graduation at the College of Dinosaurs"—
read-through (30 min.)
Finishing Up (15 min.)

SECOND DAY
Getting Started: Parents' Day Invitations (15 min.)
Story Time: Book about dinosaurs (15 min.)
Library Time: Film on dinosaurs; "Library Song" (15 min.)
Dinosaur Games: "Dinosaur Book Exchange" (15 min.)
Dinosaur Crafts: Paint Dinosaur Cave Stage (30 min.)
Washup and Snack: Veggies, dinosaur dip, potato chips, V-8 (10 min.)
Dinosaur Drama: "Graduation Day"—practice (30 min.)
Finishing Up (15 min.)

THIRD DAY
Getting Started: Digger and Dee Dee Paper Dolls (15 min.)
Story Time: Book about dinosaurs (15 min.)
Library Time: Sleuthing Out the Card Catalog (15 min.)
Dinosaur Games: "Dinosaur Rap" (15 min.)
Dinosaur Crafts: Paint Dinosaur T-shirts (30 min.)
Washup and Snack: Animal crackers, chocolate milk (15 min.)
Dinosaur Drama: "Graduation Day"—dress rehearsal
Finishing Up (15 min.)

FOURTH DAY
Getting Started: Dinosaur Bookmarks (15 min.)
Story Time: Book about dinosaurs (15 min.)
Dinosaur Crafts: Easy Dinosaur Stickpuppets (30 min.)
Dinosaur Games: "The Dinosaur Stomp" (15 min.)
Apply Dinosaur Make-up (15 min.)
Washup and Snack: Dinosaur cake, Kool-aid (15 min.)
Dinosaur Drama: Present "Graduation Day" (30 min.)
Finishing Up (15 min.)

Professor Ology finds a dinosaur egg in "Graduation Day at the College of Dinosaurs" (pages 128–135).

Grades 1–4, Long Program: First Day

Materials Checklist

____ dinosaur name tags (from this book)—have a few extra
____ yarn for name tags
____ crayons and markers
____ white cardboard for name tag backing (optional)
____ scissors
____ white glue
____ books about dinosaurs for Story Time and Library Time
____ green and red construction paper (colors optional)
____ dinosaur cookies
____ fruit punch
____ paper cups
____ paper napkins
____ copies of "Graduation Day at the College of Dinosaurs" script (from this book)
____ sheet of tin or drum for "The Dinosaur Rap"
____ words to "The Dinosaur Rap" (from this book)
____ words to "A Library Song" (from this book)
____ plastic or cardboard big dinosaur bone
____ stapler
____ paper punch
____ diplomas
____ props for play (see page 128)

The Program

Goals

Digging deep into books; know your library.

Preparation

Photocopy the dinosaur name tags on pages 122 and 124—one for each child. You may wish to further prepare tags for Grades 1–2 (see "Getting

Started"). Also copy "A Library Song" (page 126) and "The Dinosaur Rap" (page 127), one for each child, and make copies of script for "Graduation Day," (pages 128–135). The four leads will each need a script. Professor Rex needs only the last part of the script. Dee Dee can learn her part without a script.

Enlarge the dinosaur name tags as hat patterns on pages 122–124 and trace them onto sturdy cardboard.

You can make dinosaur cookies—dinosaur cutters are available. But store-bought cookies will also do.

Getting Started   (Two groups,* 15 minutes)

The children are divided into two "dinosaur caves" or circles at opposite ends of the room. Grades 1–2 are Brontosauruses and Grades 3–4 are Stegosauruses.

Dinosaur name tags are given to each group. The children write their names on the tags and color them. They cut out the tags. (Optional: Paste the name tags on cardboard for a backing, and cut out the cardboard.) Punch two holes at the top of the dinosaur tag and poke yarn through. Tie the two ends of yarn together. This slips over the child's head.

It may work best if Grades 1–2 have help with their name tags or if the librarian makes them ahead of time, and they only write their names and color. Grades 3–4 will like making the entire name tags. Black markers will make the names stand out.

Do a *Dinosaur Roll Call*: In their dinosaur caves, the children have a dinosaur roll call. They stand and say their names in loud dinosaur voices, adding either "Brontosaurus" or "Stegosaurus" to their first names. *Example*: "I am Jane Brontosaurus," or, "I am Jim Stegosaurus." Then the children say together, "We are in the _____ Library. We are the Library Dinosaurs."

Story Time   (One group, 15 minutes)

The two dinosaur groups join together for Story Time. They sit on the floor around the librarian's chair. The librarian reads them a story about dinosaurs. (See Dinosaur Book List.) The librarian tells the children how exciting it is to be able to dig deep into books and discover a good story.

---

*"Two groups" notation signifies that division of a large group is appropriate or desirable. You may prefer not to divide smaller groups.

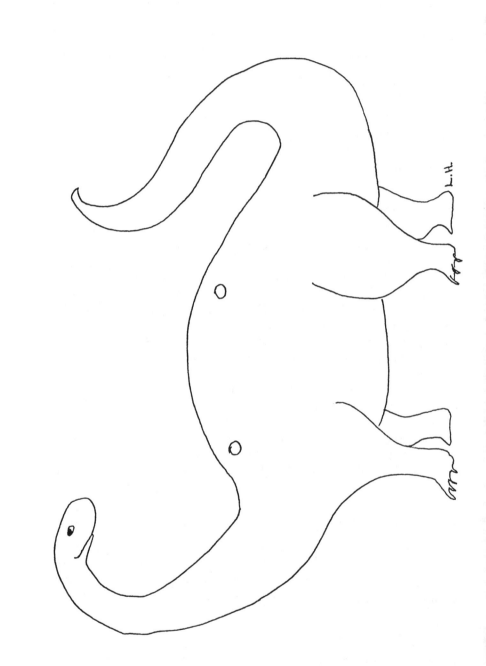

122

Library Time   (One group, 15 minutes)

Talk about the library. See how many things you can think of that are in a library. (*Examples:* Books, book stacks, card catalog, computer, pencils, stuffed animals, etc.)

Talk about Library Cards. Ask: How many have a Library Card? Talk about being a good leader and show good library habits when in the library. Talk about being a good follower and obeying the rules of the library.

Take a tour of the library. The children are divided into two groups. The group which is not touring reads "A Library Song."

Dinosaur Games   (One group, 15 minutes)

"Drop the Dinosaur Bone." The children are the dinosaurs. They stand in a circle facing the center. One child, or dinosaur, is chosen to be the bone carrier. This dinosaur carries a large dinosaur bone made from cardboard or plastic. The bone carrier drops the bone behind one of the dinosaurs. That dinosaur picks up the bone and tries to catch the original bone carrier before he reaches the open place in the circle. If the bone carrier is caught, he has to go to the center of the circle. If the dinosaur bone carrier reaches the open space safely, he stays there and the one who failed to catch him becomes bone carrier. The game is repeated.

Dinosaur Crafts   (Two groups, 30 minutes)

Dinosaur Hats. You may use enlarged dinosaur name tags on pages 122 and 124 as patterns. The Brontosaurus have green hats and the Stegosaurus have red hats. (colors optional.) Trace the brontosaurus hat pattern on green construction paper and cut out. Trace the stegosaurus hat pattern on red construction paper and cut out. The hats are stapled together.

These dinosaur hats will be worn in the play. Make sure children write their names inside them.

Washup   (One group at a time, 5 minutes)

The Brontosauruses go first, followed by the Stegosauruses. The children who finish their crafts first, go first.

Opposite: Brontosaurus name tag.

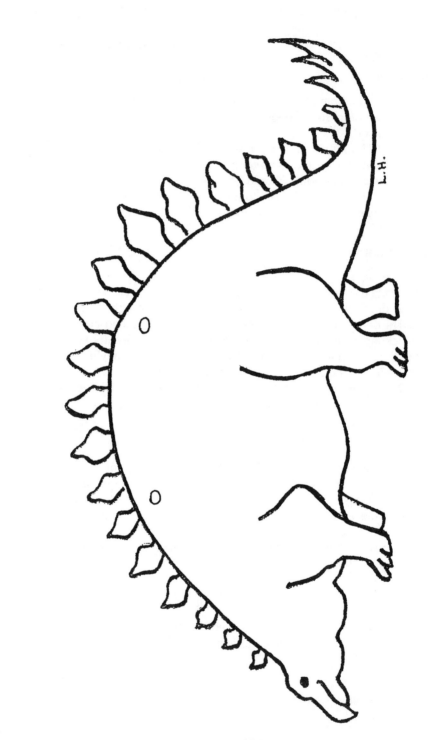

Snack   (One group, 10 minutes)

Dinosaur cookies and fruit punch.

Drama   (One group, 30 minutes)

Read through the play "Graduation Day at the College of Dinosaurs." Assign parts and stand-ins. Start acting out the play.

Note: If there is not sufficient time to learn parts, the librarian can read the play and have the characters pantomime the story.

Finishing Up   (Two groups, 15 minutes)

Do "The Dinosaur Rap."

Explain that the last session will be Parents' Day, when parents and friends are invited to see the play. Tell the children they will make invitations next time you meet.

Collect dinosaur name tags and hats. The actors take scripts home to learn their parts.

Opposite: Stegosaurus name tag.

125

A Library Song (Chant)

by

Taffy Jones

Beat out the beat with wooden blocks or other musical instruments. Chant the words.

I've got time to go to the library.
Tic toc, tic toc.

Time to read a book—agree?
Tic toc, tic toc.

Time to read and time to learn.
Tic toc, tic toc.

To read is my concern.
Tic toc, tic toc, tic.

Books, books, books, you see,
Stacks of books around me.
Fiction, fact and fable,
I read all that I am able.

Books, books, books in rhyme
Books of every kind,
Check 'em out; return on time.
Books are for my mind.

The Dinosaur Rap

by

Brian Taft Jones

(Hand claps, drum beats, or thunder rolls can be used for the beats.)

Beat—beat
500 million years ago,
Dinosaurs wandered to and fro,
Beat—beat

Beat—beat
Some two-ton bodies
In two-ounce brains
Roaring by like big freight trains
Beat—beat

Beat—beat
Why did those dudes disappear so fast?
When they were built, built to last.
Beat—beat.

Beat—beat
Over the years those dinosaur bones
Fossilized as hard as stones
Beat—beat

Beat—beat
500 million years ago
Dinosaurs wandered to and fro
Jumping lizards they were big
Now they are only left to dig
Beat—beat

Graduation Day
at the College of Dinosaurs

A Children's Library Play
by
Taffy Jones

Characters:

STEGGIE—A student
BRONTE—Another student
PROFESSOR OLOGY—Professor of archeology
DIGGER—A student
DEE DEE—Digger's little sister
PRESIDENT REX—President of the college

Note: Characters can be either sex. "Digger" paper doll, to be used in a later activity, is a boy.

Props:

red Stegosaurus hat and green makeup for Steggie
green Brontosaurus hat and green makeup for Bronte
big egg and big bone, buried under some burlap (along with other joke props—see setting notes)
two shovels
old shoe
funny pink underwear, such as an old-fashioned corset
small brush
long rope
pith helmet, glasses (optional), mustache, shorts, knee socks, heavy shoes, big hankie for Professor Ology. He [she] can wear a funny nose, [mustache] and glasses mask.
t-shirt with a dinosaur on it for Digger. He [she] adds green makeup later for graduation.
Dinosaur costume with green makeup for Dee Dee

playing cards
tin or metal for thunder sound effect
two gold awards—big round disks with a hole in the top for yarn or ribbon
  to go through. Disks are of plywood or cardboard and painted gold.
dinosaur hats and green makeup for students
diplomas—white paper with dinosaur stickers or gold seals. "College of
  Dinosaurs," date and name of student are on the diploma.
drums
tape or record of "Pomp and Circumstance" (optional) or other graduation
  march

Note: dinosaur makeup consists of green circles on cheeks and around eyes.

The play takes place at the Big Dig site at the College of Dinosaurs. Pails,
shovels, brushes are around. Graduation exercises are being held there.
Chairs have been set up in rows at the center of the site. The digging area
is to the right of the site. Burlap, or cloth, or brown paper hides the dinosaur
bone and egg, an old shoe, funny pink underwear, and any other funny
discoveries, such as a wig (could this be dinosaur hair?) and plastic wig
holder (that's not a dinosaur egg, you bonehead).
  Steggie and Bronte enter.

STEGGIE:	Hi, Bronte.
BRONTE:	Hi, Steggie.
STEGGIE:	Ready for graduation today?
BRONTE:	Ready as I'll ever be.
STEGGIE:	Will your family be here?
BRONTE:	They wouldn't miss seeing their daughter [son] graduate. Is your family coming?
STEGGIE:	They are. I expect Professor Ology will win the "Great Digging Award."
BRONTE:	He [she] has won it for the last eight years. I guess he will win it again.
STEGGIE:	What's he winning it for this year?
BRONTE:	I heard that he discovered a *dinosaur track* right here on the college campus.
STEGGIE:	That's something! He deserves to win the award.
BRONTE:	That he does.
STEGGIE:	See you at graduation, Bronte.
BRONTE:	See you, Steggie. (*Bronte exits to the left and Steggie exits to the right.*)

DIGGER:	(*Enters. He [she] is crying. He turns a pail upside down and sits on it. He cries very loud.*)
PROF.:	(*Enters, sees Digger crying.*) Digger, you are crying?
DIGGER:	Yes, Professor Ology, I am crying.
PROF.:	Why are you crying?
DIGGER:	I'm crying—because I'm crying. (*Cries harder.*)
PROF.:	Tell me, Digger, why are you crying?
DIGGER:	I am crying because I dug all semester and I never came up with anything important.
PROF.:	Now, my boy. Don't you remember what I am always teaching? (*Picks up shovel.*) You've got to dig deep and dig big. You've got to dig, dig, dig.
DIGGER:	I remember what you talked about, but all my digging didn't do me any good. I dug deep and I dug big. And I got nothing, nothing, nothing.
PROF.:	You've got to *keep* digging. (*Holds out his shovel.*) Here, Digger, get digging. (*Gives shovel to Digger and picks up another shovel and starts digging.*) (*Sings.*) You've got to dig big. You've got to dig big. You've got to dig big. Dig, dig, dig, dig, dig.
DIGGER:	(*Digs—then speaks excitedly.*) I've hit something, Professor. I've got something!
PROF.:	Go easy, Digger. Let me see what you have dug up.
DIGGER:	(*Holds up an old shoe.*) It's only an old shoe. (*Throws shoe away.*) Wouldn't you know. I dug up an old, dumb shoe.
PROF.:	Now, don't let that get you down, Digger. This time a shoe. Next time, who knows?
DIGGER:	It will be the other dumb shoe.
PROF.:	That's no way to talk. You've got to keep digging. Pick up that shovel and dig! (*Sings.*) You've got to dig big—You've got to dig big. You've got to dig, dig, dig, dig, dig. Sing, Digger.
DIGGER:	(*Starts off slowly and then sings loudly with the professor.*)
PROF.	(*Stops singing.*) What do you know? I've hit something.
DIGGER:	What did you find, Professor Ology? (*Goes to Professor.*)

130

PROF.: I don't know. (*Leans down.*) It looks like something pink. Does it look pink to you?

DIGGER: It looks pink to me.

PROF.: (*Holds up an old-fashioned corset or any other funny pink underwear.*)

DIGGER: What is that?

PROF.: Never mind, Digger. It's not worth mentioning. (*Throws the underwear down.*) (*Sternly.*) Get back to digging. (*They dig and sing.*)

DIGGER: Great digging today, Professor Ology. My shovel hit something again, Professor! I dug up a *big* bone! Come quick!

PROF.: (*Goes to Digger.*) Tyrannosaurus! Yes, you did, Digger. Here, let me take a closer look. (*Looks at bone very carefully.*) Digger—

DIGGER: Yes, Professor Ology?

PROF.: That bone—that bone you just dug up, might be— It might be a—

DIGGER: It might be a what?

PROF.: It might be a dinosaur bone. Yes, it is. You have dug up a *dinosaur* bone.

DIGGER: A dinosaur bone! Wow! Oh, wow! Now *I* will win the "Great Digging Award."

PROF.: That's a possibility.

DIGGER: I can't believe I dug up a *real* dinosaur bone. Golly! Oh, say, Professor Ology, I almost forgot I have to pick up my little sister, Dee Dee, at school. Her class had a costume party and I promised Mom.

PROF.: Run along, Digger. I will label and wrap your find most carefully, and take it to the museum to be registered for the "Great Digging Award."

DIGGER: Gee, thanks, Professor. See you later. (*Runs off.*)

PROF.: (*Sits on a pail.*) Can you beat that? That nutty kid dug up a dinosaur bone. Naturally, a dinosaur bone will win over my dinosaur track. That means this year's "Great Digging Award" won't be mine. (*Starts to cry.*) I have won the "Great Digging Award" for the last eight years. Oh, I can't bear it! (*He cries very hard. After a time, he blows his nose loudly on a big hankie.*) I should not be crying. What did I just tell Digger? I told him, no matter what, to keep

131

digging. All right—I will dig again, and maybe I will dig up something even greater than Digger's dinosaur bone. (*Digs and sings the digging song. He digs some more, then yells.*) Tyrannosaurus! I have hit something! And it looks like a big egg. (*Brushes the egg.*) It *is* a big egg. (*He holds up the egg.*) It is a dinosaur egg. I have dug up an ancient dinosaur egg. Now I, without a doubt, will win the "Great Digging Award." (*He walks back and forth with the dinosaur egg. He stumbles and almost drops the egg.*) Tyrannosaurus! I almost dropped the egg. (*Stops.*) Say—if I could hatch this dinosaur egg, I would not only win this year's "Great Digging Award," but I would be famous! I would be on TV. I would write a book and I would be rich. (*He looks at the egg.*) I wish there was a mother dinosaur around, but there hasn't been a mother dinosaur around in millions of years. I guess, if I want this egg hatched, I will have to hatch it myself. (*He lays the egg down very carefully and then with great care, he settles himself over the egg.*)

DIGGER:	(*Enters with Dee Dee, who is wearing a dinosaur costume. She stands behind Professor.*) What ya doing, Professor Ology?
PROF:	I am hatching an egg.
DIGGER:	An egg?
PROF.:	Yes, I am hatching a dinosaur egg.
DIGGER:	Wow! Oh! Wow! Did you just dig it up?
PROF.:	That I did.
DIGGER:	Gosh! Now *you* will win the "Great Digging Award."
PROF.:	That I will.
DIGGER:	How long does it take to hatch a baby dinosaur?
PROF.:	Since I never hatched one before, who knows?
DIGGER:	Want to play "Dinosaur Cards" while we wait?
PROF.:	We might as well. (*They play cards.*) (*Professor yells "Tyrannosaurus! I won," every time he wins.*)
DIGGER:	It's no fun playing with you, you always win.
PROF.:	Think positive, my boy. Think positive. (*Puts cards down.*) I'm bushed. Think I will take a snooze.
DIGGER:	Aren't you afraid you will bust the egg?

132

PROF.:	Naw! I'm only perched on it.
DIGGER:	(*Under his breath.*) He's some bird.
PROF.:	(*Snores.*)
DIGGER:	(*Yawns.*) I'm getting tired but I want to stick around and see the dinosaur hatch. (*He goes to sleep, then wakes up.*) Is it hatched yet?
PROF.:	(*Wakes up.*) No, it's not hatched yet.
DIGGER:	(*Goes to sleep again and wakes up.*) Is the egg hatched yet?
PROF.:	(*Crossly.*) No, the egg is not hatched yet.
DIGGER:	(*Goes to sleep again and wakes up.*) Is the dinosaur egg hatched yet?
PROF.:	(*Very cross.*) I said, the dinosaur egg is not hatched yet. (*He raises himself and looks at the egg. He sees Dee Dee's legs.*) Tyrannosaurus! I did it! I hatched a baby dinosaur. (*He picks up a rope and ties it around Dee Dee's waist. Dee Dee runs off pulling Professor Ology, who hangs on to the end of the rope. It is planned in the running that all the props are knocked over.*)
DIGGER:	Stop, Professor! Take that rope off my sister.
PROF.:	(*Stops suddenly.*) Your sister?
DIGGER:	That's my sister you have tied up.
PROF.:	Oh, no!
DEE DEE:	(*Rushes to the egg.*) My egg! (*Picks up egg.*)
PROF.:	That's her egg?
DIGGER:	It's her big dinosaur toy egg.
PROF.:	(*Yells.*) Tyrannosaurus! (*And faints.*)
DIGGER:	Dee Dee come here and help me wake up Professor Ology. (*They shake Professor and finally get him to his feet.*)
PROF.:	What a day! What a dig-astrophy! (*Shakes his head and mutters, "What a digastrophy!" over and over.*)
DIGGER:	(*Picks up his bone. Walks off behind the Professor.*)
PROF.:	(*Follows Digger.*)

Steggie enters from stage right. Bronte enters from stage left. They meet in the center.

STEGGIE:	Hurry, the graduation exercises are starting.
BRONTE:	I'm coming. (*They exit together.*)

Library Dinosaurs

MUSIC:	(*Tape.*) *"Pomp and Circumstance"* (*optional*). (*Thunder effect made by shaking or tapping tin.*)
STUDENTS:	(*Enter wearing dinosaur hats and dinosaur makeup. They walk slowly to the music to their chairs.*)
PRES. REX:	(*Enters wearing robe and mortarboard.*)
STUDENTS:	(*Are seated.*)
PRES. REX:	We welcome you to the 150th Graduation Exercises at the College of Dinosaurs. We will open today's ceremony by singing our alma mater, "The Dinosaur Rap."
STUDENTS:	(*All do "The Dinosaur Rap."*)
PRES. REX:	And now, Professor Ology, eight-time winner of the prestigious "Great Digging Award," will give the Commencement Address.
PROF.:	(*Goes to lecture stand.*) Students, parents and fellow professors. I have one thing, and only one thing to say to you today. Remember, when the digging gets tough, the tough get digging. You've got to dig big; you got to dig deep, and keep on digging. Thank you. (*He goes back to his chair.*)
STUDENTS:	(*Clap.*)
PRES. REX:	We have come to the time everyone has been waiting for. I am proud to present the college's famous "Great Digging Award." This year's award goes to Digger Keenan for discovering a dinosaur bone here at the College of Dinosaurs.
AUDIENCE:	(*Clap.*)
DIGGER:	(*Goes up and receives a huge gold medal.*)
PRES. REX:	(*Places the medal on a ribbon over Digger's head.*) Congratulations, Digger. (*Shakes Digger's hand.*)
DIGGER:	Thank you. (*Goes back to his chair.*)
PRES. REX:	And now for a surprise. This year, we have two "Great Digging Awards." The second "Great Digging Award" goes to our own Professor Ology, eight-time winner of this prestigious award, for discovering dinosaur tracks here at the College of Dinosaurs.
STUDENTS:	(*Clap.*)
PROF.:	(*Goes for his award.*)
PRES. REX:	(*Puts the gold medal over Professor's head.*) Congratulations, Professor Ology.
PROF.:	Thank you, President Rex. (*He returns to his seat.*)

PRES. REX: We have nothing but winners here at the College of Dinosaurs, ladies and gentlemen. I am proud to say every member of this year's graduating class is a winner. To these winners go hard-earned diplomas. Will each graduate come forward, as his or her name is called?

(Diplomas are given out. Students receive their diplomas and return to their chairs.)

PRES. REX: We have come to the end of the 150th Graduation Exercises at the College of Dinosaurs. Remember what Professor Ology always says, "When the digging gets tough, the tough get digging." Thank you.

MUSIC: *("Pomp and Circumstance" and/or drums and/or thunder as graduates exit. Then they run back, shout "Dinosaurs," and throw their dinosaur hats into the air.)*

The End

Grades 1–4, Long Program: Second Day

Materials Checklist

___ dinosaur name tags (from previous day)

___ index cards, or dinosaur copied from this book, for Parents' Day invitations

___ markers and crayons

___ scissors

___ white glue

___ dinosaur stickers for invitations (optional)

___ book about dinosaurs

___ film about dinosaurs

___ words to "A Library Song"

___ dinosaur books for Book Exchange

___ cave stage (see pages 137–138)

___ paint for cave stage

___ veggies

___ dip

___ potato chips

___ V-8 juice

___ paper cups

___ paper napkins

___ scripts for the play, "Graduation Day at the College of Dinosaurs"

___ tin sheet or drum for "The Dinosaur Rap"

___ words to "The Dinosaur Rap"

___ dinosaur hats (from previous day)

___ props for play (see page 128)

The Program

Goals

To learn more about dinosaurs, and to work together getting ready for the play.

Preparation

Make Cave Stage (illustrated on page 138). The cave stage is made out of heavy cardboard, beaver board, or thin plywood. There are three sections—the front opening of the cave stage and the two sides. The front opening (roughly 12" x 16") of the cave stage and the two sides are painted like big stones, using black, blue and white paints, or orange, beige and brown colors. (The colors are optional.) The children will paint these.

The sides of the cave stage are fastened together with 2" wide tape. Leave a small space between the front opening section and the sides and place tape over this space. This allows the sections to be opened and closed. Staple tape to the front opening section and again to the side sections.

Optional: Blocks of wood are glued to the other sides of the back of the opening section. Each block has a hole drilled through it so a dowel, about 1/2", can be pushed through. Before you insert this dowel into the hole, add a burlap curtain to the dowel. Hem the top of the curtain, about 2", for the dowel to go through. After the dowel and curtain are in place, wrap rubber bands around the ends of the dowel so the curtain cannot slip off. The curtain should measure from the dowel to about 2" below the stage opening.

Getting Started (Two groups, 15 minutes)

Give out name tags, then make Parents' Day invitations. Each child has an index card (or use a photocopied dinosaur picture from this book). They stick a dinosaur sticker (can be bought at stationery stores) or draw a dinosaur on the plain side of the card, and write: "You are invited to Parents' Day." On the lined side they write place, date, and time.

Story Time (One group, 15 minutes)

The two dinosaur groups join together for Story Time. They sit on the floor around the librarian's chair. The librarian reads them a story about dinosaurs. (See Dinosaur Book List.)

Library Time (One group, 15 minutes)

Show a film about dinosaurs. Do "A Library Song."

Dinosaur Games (One group, 15 minutes)

Play "Dinosaur Book Exchange." Each child selects a book about dinosaurs from a group that the librarian has picked out ahead of time. Then

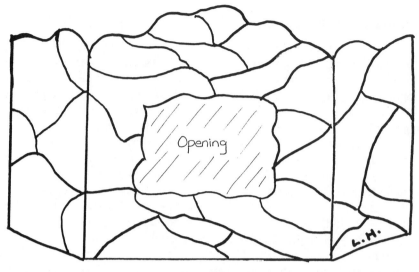

Cave Stage

they sit in a circle and read their books. When the librarian claps hands and says, "Change," each child passes his or her book to the left. They read this book until the librarian claps hands again. A drum, tambourine, or a sheet of tin can be used instead of handclapping. One or two children tell a story combining the books they have read. The stories will sound funny.

Dinosaur Crafts   (Two groups, 30 minutes)

Paint Dinosaur Cave Stage. Use red, brown, and yellow paints, or black and white paints. Have the children decorate the front of the stage like a cave. Small cans of enamel paint are good. The stage has been put together ahead of time. (See "Preparation.")

Put on some "dinosaurish" music. One or two children take a paint brush and, when the music starts, stick their brushes into one color of paint. They paint the cave stage (only small strokes and circles) until the music stops. Then the next children take the paint brushes and have turns painting the cave stage. This is repeated until each child has a turn painting or until the cave stage is finished. A drum or piece of tin can be used instead of a tape or record.

The back of the stage is also painted, so as many as six children can paint at once. Try to blend the paint for a stone effect.

Washup   (One group at a time, 5 minutes)

Snack   (Two groups, 10 minutes)

Veggies, "dinosaur dip," potato chips and V-8 juice

Drama   (One group, 30 minutes)

Rehearse play, "Graduation Day at the College of Dinosaurs." Do "The Dinosaur Rap."

Finishing Up   (Two groups, 15 minutes)

Finish the Parents' Day invitations; talk about Parents' Day. Ask each child to bring a T-shirt (white with no artwork is best) to make dinosaur T-shirts next time.

Collect dinosaur name tags and hats.

Grades 1–4, Long Program: Third Day

Materials Checklist

____ dinosaur name tags (from previous days)
____ dinosaur hats (from previous days)
____ Dee Dee paper dolls (from this book) for each child—have a few extra
____ white cardboard for backing of paper dolls (optional)
____ white glue
____ scissors
____ dinosaur book selection
____ copies of "The Dinosaur Rap"
____ a few white T-shirts (for those who forgot to bring one from home)
____ dinosaurs for T-shirts
____ acrylic paint and brushes
____ animal crackers
____ chocolate milk
____ paper cups
____ paper napkins
____ copies of the play, "Graduation Day at the College of Dinosaurs"
____ drum or tin sheet
____ props for play (see page 128)
____ rags
____ paper towels
____ paint thinner

The Program

Goal

To see that there are many different books about the same subject.

Preparation

Photocopy the Dee Dee paper doll and clothes, pages 141 and 142. Photocopy any dinosaurs from this book or elsewhere to use for T-shirt patterns.

Dee Dee paper doll and clothes

141

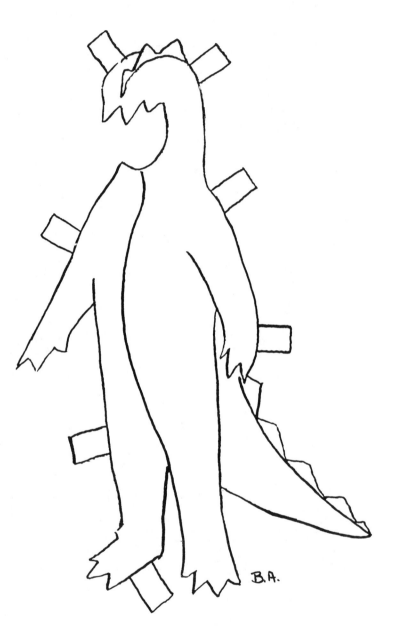

Dee Dee's dinosaur costume

Getting Started (Two groups, 15 minutes)

Give out dinosaur name tags and Dee Dee paper dolls. Children color the paper dolls and clothes. They can paste the paper dolls on white cardboard (optional). Cut out the clothes. Remember, don't cut off the tabs.

Story Time (One group, 15 minutes)

The two dinosaur groups join together for Story Time. They sit on the floor around the librarian's chair. The librarian reads them a story about dinosaurs. (See Dinosaur Book List.)

Library Time (One group, 15 minutes)

The children find books about dinosaurs. They read their book, then they show and tell about their book. See how many different books there are on the same subject.

Dinosaur Games (One group, 15 minutes)

Do "The Dinosaur Rap."

Dinosaur Crafts (Two groups, 30 minutes)

Dinosaur T-Shirts. Each child brings a T-shirt (white is best with no art work). Have T-shirts on hand for forgetters. Fill in with acrylic paint. Use black paint for eyes and details. Keep the T-shirts and lay them out to dry. They will be used in the play for Parents' Day.

Have rags, paper towels and paint thinner for cleanup.

Washup (One group at a time, 5 minutes)

Snack (One group, 10 minutes)

Animal crackers and chocolate milk.

Drama   (One group, 30 minutes)

Dress rehearsal for "Graduation Day at the College of Dinosaurs."
Do "The Dinosaur Rap."

Finishing Up   (Two groups, 15 minutes)

Finish the Dee Dee paper dolls.
Collect name tags and hats.

Grades 1–4, Long Program: Fourth Day

Materials Checklist

____ dinosaur name tags (from previous days)
____ dinosaur hats (from previous days)
____ dinosaur T-shirts (from previous day)
____ white cardboard for dinosaur bookmarks and stickpuppets
____ scissors
____ white glue
____ stapler
____ dinosaur stickers
____ yarn (optional)
____ markers and crayons
____ dinosaur book selection
____ tongue depressors, Popsicle sticks, or straws for stickpuppets
____ green makeup (green eyeshadow or theatrical makeup)
____ dinosaur cake
____ Kool-aid
____ paper cups
____ paper napkins
____ props, costumes, scripts for play, "Graduation Day at the College of Dinosaurs" (see page 128)
____ chairs for audience
____ tin sheet or drum
____ dinosaurs for stickpuppets (from this book)
____ cleansing cream
____ tissues
____ mirrors
____ bobby pins
____ "The Dinosaur Rap" sheets
____ "A Library Song" sheets

The Program

Goal

To present play for audience.

145

Dinosaur stickpuppets

Preparation

Enlarge the dinosaur stickpuppet drawing on page 146 and make several copies of each. Set up chairs for Parents' Day audience.

Getting Started   (Two groups, 15 minutes)

Give out name tags.

Make Dinosaur Bookmarks. The children cut rectangles from white cardboard for bookmarks. (Colored cardboard can also be used.) They stick a dinosaur sticker on the front of the bookmarks and write their names on them. The children can also draw their own dinosaur on the bookmark, if they prefer, and then color it. Any of the dinosaurs in this book can be reduced to a small size suitable for the bookmarks. A yarn tassel may be added at the top.

Story Time   (One group, 15 minutes)

The two dinosaur groups join together for Story Time. They sit on the floor around the librarian's chair. The librarian reads them a story about dinosaurs. (See Dinosaur Book List.)

Dinosaur Crafts   (Two groups, 30 minutes)

Easy Dinosaur Stickpuppets. Children pick out the photocopied dinosaur drawings they prefer and color them. (One per child.) Paste the drawing to cardboard, then cut out cardboard in same shape. Paste a tongue depressor, straw or popsicle stick about 1" up inside the two dinosaur pieces. Glue in place. Then glue the edges of the dinosaur pieces together. The stick is then firmly in place.

Have the stickpuppets perform on the cave stage. The children bring the stickpuppets with them to the graduation exercises during the play.

Dinosaur Games   (One group, 15 minutes)

"Dinosaur Stomp." Use a sheet of tin for thunder and drums. The children act like dinosaurs stomping. They choose a dinosaur to stomp with, then move to another dinosaur to stomp around.

147

Apply Dinosaur Makeup   (Two groups, 15 minutes)

The children put green dinosaur makeup on their cheeks in big circles. They also add some to their eyelids and make circles around their eyes.

Washup   (One group at a time, 5 minutes)

Snack   (Two groups, 10 minutes)

Dinosaur cake (any cake) and Kool-aid

Drama   (One group, 30 minutes)

Present the play "Graduation Day at the College of Dinosaurs" for parents and friends. Parents may take pictures.

Finishing Up   (Two groups, 15 minutes)

Some children will want to take off their makeup, so have cleansing cream, tissues, and helpers on hand.

The children take home dinosaur name tags, crafts, etc. Tell the children what fine dinosaurs they were. Ask them what they liked best about the program. Tell the children to come to the library, as it is their special place. Ask them if they want to take out a book on dinosaurs.

Check library cards.

Library Dinosaurs:
Grades 1–4, Short Program
Time: Two Days; 1 1/2 hours each day

FIRST DAY

Getting Started: Dinosaur name tags and bookmarks (10 min.)
Story Time: Book about dinosaurs (10 min.)
Library Time: Library tour (10 min.)
Dinosaur Games: "Drop the Dinosaur Bone" (5 min.)
Dinosaur Crafts: Dinosaur Necklaces (15 min.)
Washup and Snack: "Dinosaur dip," potato chips and V-8 juice (15 min.)
Dinosaur Drama: "Who's the Fiercest?"—read-through (20 min.)
Finishing Up: Parents' Day invitations (5 min.)

SECOND DAY

Getting Started: Dinosaur hats (10 min.)
Story Time: Book about dinosaurs (10 min.)
Library Time: Film about dinosaurs (10 min.)
Dinosaur Crafts: Easy dinosaur stickpuppets (15 min.)
Apply Dinosaur Makeup: (5 min.)
Washup and Snack: Dinosaur cookies and fruit punch (15 min.)
Dinosaur Drama: Present "Who's the Fiercest?" (20 min.)
Finishing Up (5 min.)

Grades 1–4, Short Program: First Day

Materials Checklist

____ dinosaur name tags (from this book)
____ cardboard backing for name tags (optional)
____ paper punch
____ markers and crayons
____ yarn for name tags and book marks
____ scissors
____ Veggie Dinosaur drawing (from this book)—each child receives one
____ cardboard or construction paper for dinosaur bookmarks
____ white glue
____ books about dinosaurs for Story Time and Library Time
____ large cardboard dinosaur bone
____ small dog bone biscuits
____ varnish
____ enamel paint
____ paint brushes
____ cord for dinosaur necklaces
____ "dinosaur dip" (any packaged dip)
____ potato chips
____ V-8
____ paper cups
____ paper napkins
____ scripts for puppet play "Who's the Fiercest?" (from this book)
____ puppets for play—use dinosaur stickpuppet (page 146)
____ cave stage (see pages 137–138)—optional
____ words to "The Dinosaur Rap" (from this book)
____ drum or tin sheet
____ index cards, or a photocopied dinosaur from this book, for Parents' Day invitations

The Program

Goal

Learn about the library.

Preparations

Photocopy Veggie Dinosaur (page 152), puppet play scripts for "Who's the Fiercest?" (pages 155–156), and words for "The Dinosaur Rap" (page 127)—each child needs one copy of everything. You may wish to further prepare name tags for Grades 1–2 (see "Getting Started," page 121.)

Make puppets for puppet play. For the dinosaurs, use the Easy Dinosaur Stickpuppet (see "Dinosaur Crafts," pages 146–147). For Mr. Mann, make a stickpuppet from the drawing on page 154. (Photocopy, color, cut out, and glue to a tongue depressor, Popsicle stick, or straw.)

Getting Started   (Two groups,* 10 minutes)

The children are in two circles or dinosaur caves. Give out dinosaur name tags. Grades 1–2 are Brontosauruses and Grades 3–4 are Stegosauruses. They write their names on the name tags and color them. (See "Getting Started," page 121, 122 and 124, for further suggestions.)

Color Veggie Dinosaur and cut out. Punch a hole at the top of Veggie's head. Push yarn through it. Tie yarn ends together. Now you have a dinosaur bookmark.

Story Time   (One group, 10 minutes)

The children sit on the floor around the librarian's chair. She reads them a story about dinosaurs. (See Dinosaur Book List.)

Library Time   (Two groups, 10 minutes)

Take a short tour of the library. While one group is touring, a book about dinosaurs is read to the other group.

Dinosaur Games   (One group, 5 minutes)

"Drop the Dinosaur Bone." See "Dinosaur Games," page 123.

---

*"Two groups" notation signifies that division of a large group is appropriate or desirable. You may prefer not to divide smaller groups.

Veggie dinosaur

Dinosaur Crafts (Two groups, 15 minutes)

Dinosaur Necklaces. Take small dog bone biscuits and paint them with acrylic or enamel paint and varnish. When dry, tie a hemp cord around the top of the first bone (each child will need four or five bones). Leave a space, then tie cord around the next bone. Do the remaining bones. Leave enough cord at the end so the cord can be tied together to make the necklace. Be sure the cord is long enough to fit over the head. The dinosaur bones can also be made out of cardboard.

Washup (Two groups, 5 minutes)

Snack (One group, 10 minutes)

Dinosaur dip (any packaged dip), potato chips and V-8 juice.

Dinosaur Drama (One group, 15 minutes)

Read through the puppet play "Who's the Fiercest?" Choose puppeteers and go through it with the puppets.

Do "The Dinosaur Rap."

Finishing Up (Two groups, 10 minutes)

Make Parents' Day invitations: Take index cards and stick dinosaur stickers to the plain side, or draw a dinosaur on it and color it. On the lined side, write "Parents' Day," and the place, date and time.

Talk to the children about Parents' Day. Tell them to invite their friends to see the play also.

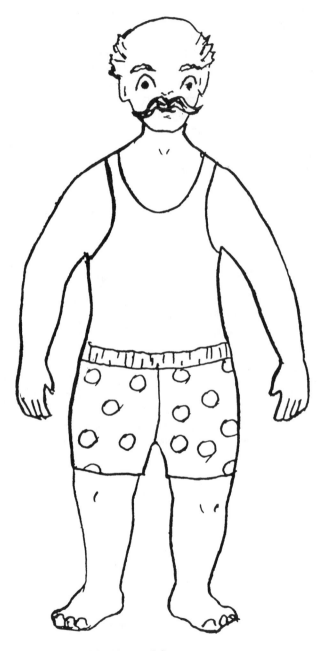

Mr. Mann stickpuppet

154

Who's the Fiercest?

A Stickpuppet Play
by
Taffy Jones

Characters:

BRONTOSAURUS (stickpuppet)
STEGOSAURUS (stickpuppet)
TYRANNOSAURUS REX (stickpuppet)
MR. MANN (stickpuppet)
CHILDREN, divided into Brontosauruses and Stegosauruses (wearing dinosaur hats)

The play takes place on the cave stage. The children are seated at the sides of the cave stage, Brontosauruses on one side, Stegosauruses on the other.

BRONT.:	(*Enters.*) I am the fiercest creature in the whole world. (*Roars.*)
STEGO.:	(*Enters.*) You are wrong, Brontosaurus. *I* am the fiercest creature in the whole world. (*Roars.*)
BRONT.:	You just think you are the fiercest. *I* am the fiercest.
STEGO.:	Wrong! Wrong! Wrong! Everyone knows that *I*, Steggie Stegosaurus, am the fiercest creature alive.
BRONT.:	Dead or alive, *I* am the fiercest animal to roam the earth.
STEGO.:	You only eat vegetables. I eat meat.
BRONT.:	But I have a long neck and weigh two tons.
STEGO.:	You trip over your own feet.
CHILDREN:	(*Enter from both sides.*)
CHILDREN STEGS.:	Stegosauruses are the fiercest!

155

CHILDREN BRONTS.:	Brontosauruses are the fiercest!
CHILDREN STEGS.:	Stegosauruses are the fiercest!
CHILDREN BRONTS.:	Brontosauruses are the fiercest!
CHILDREN STEGS.:	Stegosauruses!
CHILDREN BRONTS.:	Brontosauruses!
CHILDREN STEGS.:	Stegosauruses!
CHILDREN BRONTS.:	Brontosauruses!

(*Thunder or banging noise like loud footsteps.*)

TYRAN. REX:	(*Enters. Loud and deep voice.*) I am Tyrannosaurus Rex, King of the Dinosaurs. *I* am the fiercest of all the dinosaurs. I am mean. I eat flesh.
STEGO.:	I am thundering out of here. (*Hides.*)
BRONT.:	Me, too. (*Hides.*)
TYRAN. REX:	(*Roars.*) I am the mightiest of the mighty, and the fiercest of the fiercest. Nobody is fiercer than me.

(*More thunder noise*)

MR. MANN:	(*Enters.*) All you monsters are wrong.
TYRAN. REX:	How can that be? *I* am the fiercest creature alive.
MR. MANN:	I am sorry to inform you that this distinction goes to me.
TYRAN. REX:	And who may you be?

(*Brontosaurus and Stegosaurus come out from hiding places.*)

BRONT.:	Who are you?
MR. MANN:	I am called — man.
TYRAN. REX:	Man? But you are so small.
STEGO:	But, you are so funny looking.
tyran. rex:	I don't believe you are the fiercest.
MR. MANN:	Believe it. I will be around long after you fellows go.
STEGO.:	I don't believe it.
BRONT.:	I don't believe it.
CHILDREN:	We believe it!

(They all do "The Dinosaur Rap.")

The End

Grades 1–4, Short Program: Second Day

Materials Checklist

____ dinosaur name tags (from previous day)
____ dinosaur hat pattern (from this book)
____ green and red construction paper (colors optional)
____ black markers
____ scissors
____ stapler
____ film about dinosaurs
____ book about dinosaurs for Story Time
____ dinosaurs for stickpuppets (from this book)
____ tongue depressors, Popsicle sticks or straws for stickpuppets
____ green makeup (eyeshadow or theatrical makeup)
____ dinosaur cookies
____ fruit punch
____ paper cups
____ paper napkins
____ copies of the puppet play "Who's the Fiercest?"
____ cave stage
____ puppets for play
____ "Dinosaur Rap" sheets
____ cleansing cream
____ tissues
____ chairs
____ mirror
____ bobby pins

The Program

Goal

To present play for audience.

Preparation

See the dinosaur hat instructions on page 123 and trace them onto sturdy cardboard. Enlarge the Easy Dinosaur Stickpuppet, page 146, and make several copies. Set up chairs for Parents' Day audience. You may wish to bake you own dinosaur cookies ahead of time—cutters and molds are available. (Otherwise, plain cookies will do.)

Getting Started   (Two groups, 10 minutes)

Make dinosaur hats. See "Dinosaur Crafts," page 123.

Story Time   (One group, 10 minutes)

Children sit around the librarian's chair for story. (See Dinosaur Book List.)

Library Time   (One group, 10 minutes)

Show a film about dinosaurs.

Dinosaur Crafts   (Two groups, 15 minutes)

Easy Dinosaur Stickpuppets. See "Dinosaur Crafts," pages 146–147. The children hold these stickpuppets in the play. These can also be used in the play in the cave stage.

Dinosaur Makeup   (Two groups, 5 minutes)

Instead of games the children make big, green circles on their cheeks with green makeup and a green line down their noses. Add green on the eyelids and make small green circles around the eyes.

Washup   (Two groups, 5 minutes)

Snack   (One group, 10 minutes)

Dinosaur cookies and fruit punch.

Dinosaur Drama (One group, 20 minutes)

Present puppet play "Who's the Fiercest?"

Finishing Up (Two groups, 5 minutes)

Remove makeup.

Tell the children what great Library Dinosaurs they were. Have them take home name tags, crafts, etc.

Tell them the library is their special place. Reading a book is fun like watching TV.

Library Dinosaurs:
Preschool–Kindergarten, Long Program
Time: 2 days; 1 1/2 hours each day

FIRST DAY
Getting Started: Dinosaur name tags, dinosaur eggs (10 min.)
Story Time: Book about dinosaurs (10 min.)
Library Time: Library tour (10 min.)
Dinosaur Games: "Dinosaur March" (5 min.)
Dinosaur Crafts: Dinosaur Hats (15 min.)
Washup and Snack: Dinosaur cookies, fruit punch (15 min.)
Dinosaur Drama: "The Dinosaur Band"—read-through (15 min.)
Finishing Up: Parents' Day Invitations (10 min.)

SECOND DAY
Getting Started: "Dinosaur Rap" (10 min.)
Story Time: Book about dinosaurs (10 min.)
Library Time: Film about dinosaurs (10 min.)
Dinosaur Games: "Find the Dinosaur Eggs" (5 min.)
Dinosaur Crafts: Baby Dinosaur Paper Doll (15 min.)
Washup and Snack: Cupcakes and juice (15 min.)
Apply Dinosaur Makeup (5 min.)
Dinosaur Drama: Present "The Dinosaur Band" (15 min.)
Finishing Up (5 min.)

Preschool–Kindergarten Long Program:
First Day

Materials Checklist

____ dinosaur name tags (from this book)
____ yarn for name tags
____ book about dinosaurs for Story Time
____ paper punch
____ dinosaur hat patterns (from this book)
____ green and red construction paper (colors optional)
____ scissors
____ stapler
____ crayons and markers
____ acrylic paint and brushes
____ plastic eggs (from L'eggs hosiery)
____ stones to put inside eggs (for musical instruments)
____ dinosaur cookies
____ fruit punch
____ paper napkins
____ paper cups
____ one copy of the play "The Dinosaur Band" (from this book)
____ musical instruments—sticks, drums, bells, etc.
____ tape or record of marching music for game, and other music for play
____ tape or record player
____ props for play (see page 164)

The Program

Goal

To learn the sections of the library.

Preparation

You will need to have collected "L'eggs" eggs beforehand. Photocopy name tag, page 122, enough copies for group. For this age group, it is best to do most of the work ahead of time, except coloring (see "Getting Started,"

161

this page). See dinosaur hat instructions, page 123, and trace onto sturdy cardboard. You may wish to make dinosaur cookies ahead of time (cutters and molds are available)—but any cookies will do.

Getting Started   (Two groups,* 10 minutes)

The children are divided into two groups or dinosaur caves at opposite ends of the room.

A dinosaur name tag is given to each child.

The children paint dinosaur eggs (L'eggs egg) with acrylic paint.

Story Time   (One group, 10 minutes)

The two dinosaur groups join together for Story Time. They sit around the librarian while a dinosaur story is read.

Library Time   (Two groups, 10 minutes)

Take a short tour of the library. While one group is touring, a book is read to the other group.

Dinosaur Games   (One group, 5 minutes)

"Dinosaur March." Play marching music on tape or record player. The dinosaurs march around the room playing the musical instruments used in the Dinosaur Band. Small stones in plastic "L'Eggs" eggs make great musical instruments.

Dinosaur Crafts   (Two groups, 15 minutes)

Dinosaur Hats. See "Dinosaur Crafts," page 123.

Washup   (One group at a time, 5 minutes)

Snack   (One group, 10 minutes)

Dinosaur cookies and fruit punch. (Save the cans for musical instruments.) Count on two cookies per child and one paper cup of fruit juice. Have extra for helpers.

*"Two groups" notation signifies that division of large groups is appropriate or desirable. You may prefer not to divide smaller groups.

Dinosaur Drama   (One group, 20 minutes)

Read through the play "The Dinosaur Band." Give each child a musical instrument. Count out a steady beat and have the children follow with their instruments. Choose the band leader. Let several children hold the baton and lead the band. Pick the most outgoing for the band conductor.

Have several children try out for the Soloist. Again, choose the one that speaks out and shows confidence.

Read through the play again with band leader and soloist.

Tell the children they can bring in any musical instruments from home to use in the play. They can be purchased or homemade.

Finishing Up   (Two groups, 10 minutes)

Make Parents' Day Invitations: Give each child an index card. On the plain side they add a dinosaur sticker, or draw a dinosaur. On the lined side, write "Parents' Day" and the place, date and time.

Tell the children to be sure to give the invitations to their parents. Remind them about musical instruments. Collect dinosaur name tags. Soloist takes play script home to learn part.

The Dinosaur Band

Characters:

THE DINOSAUR CONDUCTOR
THE DINOSAUR BAND (children)
SOLOIST

Props:

musical instruments
chairs
music stand with music
baton
dinosaur hats
green dinosaur makeup
fake (or real) microphone for soloist
tails or tuxedo, or bow tie, for conductor (optional)

The children wear their dinosaur hats and green dinosaur makeup. They have different dinosaur musical instruments, such as a large juice can with string attached through holes in the sides of the can for a handle. Punch two holes opposite each other at the top of the can. Run a string about 14" long through these holes and tie. Use a stick to beat the can to produce nice steady tones. Hold the string of the can while beating it. Other good instruments include two sticks of wood about 7" or 8" long and 1" wide to hit together, two pie tins to hit together, drums, bells, triangles, tambourines, etc.

The children take their places in chairs set up facing the audience. They sit and tune up their dinosaur instruments, making a terrible noise. Then the dinosaur band conductor comes in very proudly with big steps to loud drum beats, or a crashing noise. The conductor stands in front of a music stand with music on it. He or she stands on a box facing the band and taps the baton (stick) on the side of the stand. There is a great pounding, beating, hitting, rattling, etc. of instruments, as the conductor directs the band.

The Dinosaur Band Conductor waves the baton about and puts on quite a show. When the conductor brings the baton down, the music stops.

SOLOIST: (*Stands in front of the band and holds a microphone.*)

CONDUCTOR: (*Holds the baton high. Waits for the band's attention. Brings the baton down sharply.*)

BAND: (*Plays until conductor stops them.*)

SOLOIST: (Sings.) If you spill your milk—read a book.

BAND: (*Plays.*)

SOLOIST: If you are afraid at night—find a light—read a book.

BAND: (*Plays.*)

SOLOIST: If you lose a friend—read a book.

BAND: (*Plays.*)

SOLOIST: If you feel shy—read a book.

BAND: (*Plays.*)

SOLOIST: If you feel bad—be glad—you can read a book.

BAND: (*Plays. They all stand up, playing their instruments and shout together:*)
               Read a book! Read a book!

Conductor brings down the baton and the music ends. The soloist bows and exits. The conductor has the band stand and bow. The conductor then bows to the audience. The band walks off. The conductor bows again and walks off.

Preschool–Kindergarten, Long Program: Second Day

Materials Checklist

____ dinosaur name tags (from previous day)
____ dinosaur hats (from previous day)
____ book about dinosaurs
____ film about dinosaurs
____ L'Eggs eggs (from previous day)—make sure there is one for each child
____ children's names on pieces of paper (to put in eggs)
____ small dinosaurs for awards (optional)
____ Dee Dee paper doll (from this book)
____ crayons and markers
____ scissors
____ white glue
____ cardboard for paper doll backing
____ cupcakes
____ fruit juice
____ paper cups
____ paper napkins
____ chairs for audience
____ props for play (see page 164)
____ green makeup (eyeshadow or theatrical makeup)
____ cleansing cream
____ tissues
____ mirror
____ bobby pins

The Program

Goals

To present play for audience, and to sharpen observation skills.

Preparation

Photocopy Dee Dee paper doll and clothes (pages 141–142) — enough for each child to have copies. Set up chairs for Parents' Day audience. You may wish to bake your own cupcakes ahead of time.

Getting Started   (Two groups, 10 minutes)

Give out dinosaur name tags.
Read "The Dinosaur Rap" to children (page 127). Have them clap along.

Story Time   (One group, 10 minutes)

Read a book about dinosaurs. (See Dinosaur Book List.)

Library Time   (One group, 10 minutes)

Show a film about dinosaurs. If time, talk about the film.

Dinosaur Games   (One group, 5 minutes)

The children are told their dinosaur eggs from yesterday are hidden around the room. Tell exactly what area so the children do not leave the room. Give them three minutes to find an egg. They look into the eggs for their names. If someone finds his or her own name, he or she is a winner. If someone finds more than one egg, he or she leaves the other egg hidden for someone else to find. They keep looking for their names for as long as there is time. In the last couple of minutes, the winners are announced. Small plastic dinosaurs that fit into the egg make good prizes. (Optional.)

Dinosaur Crafts   (Two groups, 15 minutes)

Dee Dee Paper Doll. Each child has a Dee Dee Paper Doll and clothes photocopied from this book. Color them. Then cut out the doll and paste to white cardboard for backing. Cut the cardboard to fit the drawing. Cut out the clothes but remember not to cut off the tabs.

Washup   (One group at a time, 5 minutes)

Snack   (One group, 10 minutes)

Cupcakes and juice. (One cupcake and one cup of juice per person.)

Dinosaur Drama   (One group, 15 minutes)

Put green dinosaur spots on children's cheeks, a green stripe down nose, and green circles around eyes. Children wear dinosaur hats. Present "The Dinosaur Band." For encore, do "The Dinosaur Rap." Have picture-taking time.

Finishing Up   (Two groups, 10 minutes)

Tell the children they were great Library Dinosaurs. Take off green makeup with tissues and cold cream. Children take home dinosaur name tags, crafts, etc.

Library Dinosaurs:
Preschool–Kindergarten, Short Program
Time: One day; 1 1/2 hours

Getting Started: Dinosaur name tags (10 minutes)
Story Time: Book about dinosaurs (10 min.)
Library Time: Library tour (10 min.)
Dinosaur Games: "Sit on the Dinosaur Track" (5 min.)
Dinosaur Crafts: Dee Dee Paper Doll (15 min.)
Washup and Snack: Dinosaur cookies, fruit punch (15 min.)
Dinosaur Drama: "The Dinosaur Rap" (20 min.)
Finishing Up (5 min.)

Materials Checklist

____ dinosaur name tags (from this book)
____ yarn for name tags
____ scissors
____ paper punch
____ white glue
____ white cardboard for name tag backing (optional)
____ book about dinosaurs
____ drum
____ chairs for game
____ paper "dinosaur track"
____ Dee Dee Paper Doll and clothes (from this book)—enough for group
____ dinosaur cookies
____ fruit punch
____ paper napkins
____ paper cups

The Program

Goal

To learn about the library and discover it's a fun place to be.

Preparation

Photocopy dinosaur name tags—use the tag on page 122. For this age group, you may wish to prepare the name tags ahead of time, leaving only coloring for children. Photocopy the Dee Dee Paper Doll and clothes, pages 141–142, enough for group. You may wish to bake you own dinosaur-shaped cookies ahead of time (molds and cutters are available), but plain store-bought cookies can be called "dinosaur" cookies. Draw a large dinosaur footprint and cut it out (for Dinosaur Games).

Getting Started   (Two groups,* 10 minutes)

The dinosaur name tags are given out to color.

Story Time   (One group, 10 minutes)

Read a book about dinosaurs.

Library Time   (Two groups, 10 minutes)

Take a short tour of the library. While one group is touring, the other group is talking about what they see in the library.

Dinosaur Games   (One group, 5 minutes)

"Sit on the Dinosaur Tracks." Chairs are set up as for musical chairs—in a line, with every other one facing the opposite way. There should be one less chair than children. The children walk around the chairs to a drum beat. In one chair is a large dinosaur track. The children try to sit on a chair when the drum beat stops. Each time the children go around the chairs, another chair is taken away. The child who sits on the dinosaur track gets a free turn to go around if he or she does not find a chair on another round.

Dinosaur Crafts   (Two groups, 15 minutes)

Dee Dee Paper Doll. See "Dinosaur Crafts," pages 141 and 142.

Washup   (One group at a time, 5 minutes)

*"Two groups" designation signifies that division of a large group is appropriate or desirable. You may prefer not to divide smaller groups.

Snack   (One group, 10 minutes)

Dinosaur cookies and fruit punch.

Dinosaur Drama   (One group, 20 minutes)

Enter in a straight line and face the audience. Each child says his or her name and bows. Then librarian reads "The Dinosaur Rap" (page 127) as the children clap their hands.

Finishing Up   (Two groups, 5 minutes)

Talk-it-over time.

Tell the children what great dinosaurs they were.

Tell the children to come to the library often, and to take out books to read in between watching TV.

Children take home dinosaur name tags, crafts, etc.

4. Library Bookworms

Library bookworms will burrow into the pleasures of reading and all the library has to offer. They will become more familiar with books in programs that discuss the difference between fiction and non-fiction, teach the parts of a book, and even give children the opportunity to write and illustrate their own books. Good library habits are emphasized through dramatics and games.

A participant in the play "The Wiggly Bookworms" (begins on page 203).

173

Library Bookworms:
Grades 1–4, Long Program
Time: 4 days; 2 1/2 hours each day

FIRST DAY
Getting Started: Bookworm name tags, roll call (15 min.)
Story Time: Fiction book about worms (fiction) (15 min.)
Library Time: Talk about worms; learn parts of a book;
read non-fiction book about worms (15 min.)
Bookworm Games: "The Bookworm Bounce" (15 min.)
Bookworm Crafts: Bookworm Paper Plate Masks (30 min.)
Washup and Snack: Cheese puffs, fruit juice (15 min.)
Bookworm Drama: "The Hatters"—read-through (30 min.)
Finishing Up: Parents' Day Invitations (15 min.)

SECOND DAY
Getting Started: Start writing story, "The Missing Oreos" (15 min.)
Story Time: Book about worms (15 min.)
Library Time: Film about worms, books, or hats (15 min.)
Bookworm Games: "The Bookworm Bounce" and "Looby Bookworm" (15 min.)
Bookworm Crafts: Bookworm Big Hats (30 min.)
Washup and Snack: Oreos and milk (15 min.)
Bookworm Drama: "The Hatters"—practice (30 min.)
Finishing Up: Finish writing story (15 min.)

THIRD DAY
Getting Started: Decorate Big Hats (15 min.)
Story Time: Book about hats (15 min.)
Library Time: Sleuthing Out the Card Catalog (15 min.)
Bookworm Games: "A Hat Fashion Show"
Bookworm Crafts: Bookworm Paper Doll (30 min.)
Washup and Snack: Veggies, dip, potato chips, V-8 (15 min.)
Bookworm Drama: "The Hatters"—dress rehearsal (30 min.)
Finishing Up: Bookworm stickpuppets (15 min.)

FOURTH DAY
Getting Started and Library Time: Illustrate "About Bookworms" (30 min.)
Story Time: Book about hats (15 min.)
Bookworm Crafts: Bookworm Mobiles (30 min.)
Washup and Snack: Cupcakes and milk (15 min.)
Bookworm Drama: Present "The Hatters" (45 min.)
Finishing Up (15 min.)

Grades 1–4, Long Program: First Day

Materials Checklist

____ bookworm name tags (from this book)—have a few extra
____ yarn for name tags and bookworm masks
____ white cardboard for name tag backing (optional)
____ scissors
____ index cards, or bookworm copied from this book, for Parents' Day invitations
____ white glue
____ stapler
____ large white paper plates
____ crayons and markers
____ tape, record or piano for music
____ tape or record player
____ tongue depressors or Popsicle sticks
____ construction paper
____ roly-poly eyes (optional)
____ book for Story Time
____ cheese puffs
____ fruit punch
____ paper cups
____ napkins
____ ten copies of play "The Hatters" (from this book)
____ props for play (see page 181)

The Program

Goal

To learn about fiction and non-fiction books, and to learn good library habits.

Preparation

Photocopy bookworm name tag (page 176) and "Bookworm Bounce" (page 178)—enough for group, plus extra. Make ten copies of the play "The

Bookworm name tag

Hatters" (pages 181–183) – four for actors, four for stand-ins, and two for the librarians. If you decide to use bookworm pictures for this book for Parents' Day invitations, make enough photocopies for each child to have at least one. You may wish to do extra preparation on name tags for Grades 1–2 (see "Getting Started").

Getting Started   (Two groups,* 15 minutes)

The children are divided into two groups or bookworm circles at opposite ends of the room. Grades 1–2 are the Master Bookworms and Grades 3–4 are the Ph.D. Bookworms. Photocopied bookworm name tags are given to each child. The children write their names on the tags, or the names can be written out ahead from the sign-up sheet. Depending on their grade, they write "Master" or "Ph.D." on the bookworm's book. They color and cut out the drawing. Then they paste the name tag on white cardboard for a backing and cut out the cardboard (optional).

Punch two holes at the top of the bookworm name tag and poke the yarn through. Tie the two ends of the yarn together. This slips over the child's head. Make yarn long enough to do this.

It may work best if Grades 1–2 have their name tags put together ahead and only write their names and color. Grades 3–4 will like to make their own name tags. Black magic markers will make the names stand out.

Now do the *Bookworm Roll Call*: Each child says his or her first name and adds "Bookworm." *Example:* "I am Laurie Bookworm," or, "I am Greg Bookworm." Have the children stand as they speak. Tell them that bookworms speak clearly and even though bookworms are small, they have strong voices. Then all the children say together, "We are in the _____ Library. We are library bookworms."

Story Time   (One group, 15 minutes)

The bookworms sit on the floor around the librarian's chair. The librarian reads them a fiction book about worms. (See Bookworm Book List.)

Library Time   (One group, 15 minutes)

Have a discussion about worms, bookworms and books. Sample questions: Where have you seen a worm? Do you like worms? Are there

---

*"Two groups" notation signifies that division of a large group is appropriate or desirable for an activity. You may prefer not to divide small groups.

good worms? What worms are good? (Earthworms.) What worms are bad? (Tent caterpillars.) Have you ever used a worm for bait? Did you like baiting your fish hook with a worm? Did you know there are real bookworms? Have you ever seen one? Are bookworms harmful to books? (Yes, they eat the paste from book bindings.)

What kind of books do you like to read? Where is a book's binding? (Where the book is put together.) Can you tell me the parts of a book? (Book jacket, book cover, flyleaf, pages, binding, spine.) Did you know? — The top of the book is called the *head*. The side that is fastened together is called the *back*. The front edge is the *fore edge* and the bottom is the *tail*. Each leaf of paper has two sides known as *pages*. Some books are for learning and other books are for fun.

Is there another kind of bookworm? (People — someone who studies and reads a lot.) Could you be a bookworm?

(Read a *non-fiction* book about worms. See Bookworm Book List.)

Bookworm Games (One group, 15 minutes)

"The Bookworm Bounce." The librarian reads the words. The children follow the actions.

LIBRARIAN:	(*Wiggles.*) Wiggle little bookworms Wiggle, wiggle.
BOOKWORMS:	(*Shake their heads, "No."*) No, No, No, No Not in the library.
LIBRARIAN:	(*Giggles.*) Giggle little bookworms Giggle, giggle.
BOOKWORMS:	No, No, No, No (*Shake heads, "No."*) Not in the library.
LIBRARIAN:	(*Sizzles — put teeth together and blow through the teeth with an "S" sound.*) Sizzle little bookworms Sizzle, sizzle.
BOOKWORMS:	No, No, No, No (*Shake heads, "No."*) Not in the library.
LIBRARIAN:	Read little bookworms, Read a good book, On a train,

On a plane,
Open a book.

Doodle little bookworms,
Doodle, doodle.

BOOKWORMS: No, No, No, No (*Shake heads, "No."*)
Not in the library.

LIBRARIAN: (*Bounces hand up and down as if dribbling a ball.*)
Dribble little bookworms,
Dribble, dribble.

BOOKWORMS: No, No, No, No. (*Shake heads, "No."*)
Not in the library.

LIBRARIAN: Be smart bookworms,
Start today,
Take a look,
Read a book
That's the way.

Bookworm Crafts (Two groups, 30 minutes)

Bookworm Paper-Plate Masks. Draw a bookworm face on a large white paper plate. Color the face. Make a construction-paper tongue. Add roly-poly eyes (optional). Take a tongue depressor or Popsicle stick and glue to the backside of the plate about 1" up the plate. This becomes the handle of the mask. You can add a collar or bow made from construction paper and glue to the stick where it meets the paper plate.

Washup (Two groups, 5 minutes)

The Master Bookworms go first, followed by the Ph.D. Bookworms. The children who finish crafts first go first.

Snack (One group, 10 minutes)

Cheese puffs (they look like worms) and fruit juice.

Bookworm Drama (One group, 30 minutes)

Read through the play "The Hatters." Choose the actors and stand-ins for the parts, and act it out.

Finishing Up   (Two groups, 15 minutes)

Collect name tags.

Remind the children about the next program. Tell them they can bring a friend. Tell the children that Parents' Day will be the last day of the program. Make invitations: use index cards (draw pictures of bookworms on them) or photocopied bookworm pictures. Write on them: "Parents' Day" and the date, time and place. Tell the actors and stand-ins to learn their lines (take scripts home). Remind them they will perform the play on Parents' Day.

The Hatters

A Children's Library Play (Grades 1–4)
by
Taffy Jones

Characters:

BIG HAT
LITTLE HAT
POINTED HAT
BAD HAT
MISS HAT, THE LIBRARIAN
ANNOUNCER

Props:

Hats made during craft period. BIG HAT wears a big hat, LITTLE HAT a little one, POINTED HAT wears a pointed one, and MISS HAT wears a fancy hat. BAD HAT wears a medium-sized hat with a band which reads "BAD HAT." This band is later replaced by one which reads "GOOD HAT." All have books. A table with five chairs is needed.

The play takes place in the _____ Library. There is a long table with three chairs at the table facing the audience and a chair at each end. That makes five chairs.

ANNOUNCER:	(*Enters and faces the audience.*) Welcome everybody. You are in the _____ Library, where there are good stories going around. I have one to tell you. It is a story about the Hatters. There is BIG HAT.
BIG HAT:	(*Enters and takes one of the first chairs facing the audience and reads a book.*)
ANNOUNCER:	Then there is LITTLE HAT.

181

LITTLE HAT:	(*Enters and takes a seat next to Big Hat. Little Hat reads a book.*)
ANNOUNCER:	And then, there is mean old, BAD HAT. (*Exits.*)
BAD HAT:	(*Runs in yelling.*) What are you dudes doing? Reading a book?
LITTLE HAT:	Sh! Don't yell in the library.
BAD HAT:	I can yell any time I want too. No LITTLE HAT can stop me. (*Jumps up on the table and yells.*)
BIG HAT:	(*Stands up.*) Get off the table, BAD HAT, and stop the noise.
BAD HAT:	Don't come any closer or I'll kick your big hat right off your big head. (*Kicks at BIG HAT.*) Your hat is too big anyways. Your big hat is always getting into people's way—*my* way! (*Turns to LITTLE HAT.*) And, your hat is too small. (*In a sing-song voice*) BIG HAT is a big hat, and LITTLE HAT is a little hat. You're too big (*Sticks out his tongue at BIG HAT.*) and you're too small. (*Makes a face at LITTLE HAT.*)
POINTED HAT:	(*Enters.*) And, you are a Bad Hat.
BAD HAT:	Look who just blew in. The Hatter with a pointed hat. Ha. Ha. You are the funniest of all. I am glad I don't have a pointed hat like you.
POINTED HAT:	And, I am glad I am not a Bad Hat like you.
BAD HAT:	Says who?
POINTED HAT:	Says me!
BIG HAT:	I say so too.
LITTLE HAT:	Me too!
POINTED HAT:	We are not going to talk to you anymore.
BAD HAT:	I don't care. Who wants to talk to you three Hatters anyway? Your hat is too big. (*Goes to BIG HAT and knocks off the hat.*) Your hat is too small (*Goes to LITTLE HAT and knocks off the hat.*) And you, (*Goes to Pointed Hat.*) You are the funniest of all. (*Walks around but the others do not speak. They keep reading their books.*) All right, if that is the way you want it, I'm leaving. Who wants to be in this library, anyway? (*Starts to walk away.*) I'm going. (*Walks away some more.*) I said, I'm leaving! (*Nobody pays attention to him.*) I'm gone. (*exits.*)
BIG HAT:	I'm glad he (she) is gone.

182

LITTLE HAT:	A hat like that doesn't belong in a library.
POINTED HAT:	BAD HAT must have problems to make him so mean.
MISS HAT:	(*Enters wearing a fancy hat.*) Hello, everybody. I have a great book to read to you today. (*Takes her place at the end of the table.*) Where is BAD HAT?
LITTLE HAT:	He (she) left, and I hope he (she) never comes back.
MISS HAT:	BAD HAT is a person who is hard to like. It is too bad BAD HAT can't be here for our new story. I know he (she) would like it very much. It's all about the MAD HATTER at a tea party. (*Opens her book.*) Once upon a time...
BAD HAT:	(*Enters quietly and sits at the other end of the table.*)
MISS HAT:	Welcome, BAD HAT. I am glad you could make it. I have the book you said you would like to hear.
BAD HAT:	Thank you, MISS HAT. (*Takes off hat and puts GOOD HAT sign in the hatband.*) I like your big hat, BIG HAT. (*Turns to LITTLE HAT.*) I like you little hat, LITTLE HAT. (*Turns to Pointed Hat.*) And, your hat looks good on you, POINTED HAT.
MISS HAT:	And your new hat, BAD HAT, makes you look very handsome.
OTHERS:	It does.
BAD HAT-GOOD HAT:	I like it too.
ANNOUNCER:	So ends the story of The Hatters in the _____ Library. We all wear different hats and are proud of the hats we wear. Bad hats are out.
OTHERS:	The end. (*They all get up and stand in a straight line facing the audience. They holds hands and bow.*)

183

Grades 1–4, Long Program: Second Day

Materials Checklist

____ bookworm name tags (from previous day)
____ cardboard cut a bit larger than typing paper. Each child will need two pieces.
____ typing paper (at least four pieces per child—have a lot of extra handy)
____ stapler
____ paper punch
____ markers or pens
____ book for Story Time
____ film about worms, books, or hats
____ Oreos
____ milk
____ paper cups
____ napkins
____ bookworm masks (from previous day)
____ cardboard or posterboard for big hats (any color)
____ scripts for play "The Hatters."
____ props for play (see page 181)

The Program

Goal

To experience writing a book.

Preparation

Photocopy the three oreo bookworms (page 185–186)—each child needs one copy of each. (Copy the two drawings on page 185 onto separate pages.) Follow instructions for the Big Hat pattern, page 188; trace onto sturdy cardboard and cut out.

[Above and opposite:] Illustrations for "The Missing Oreos." Copy drawings above onto separate sheets, or have children cut them apart and tape onto separate sheets.

185

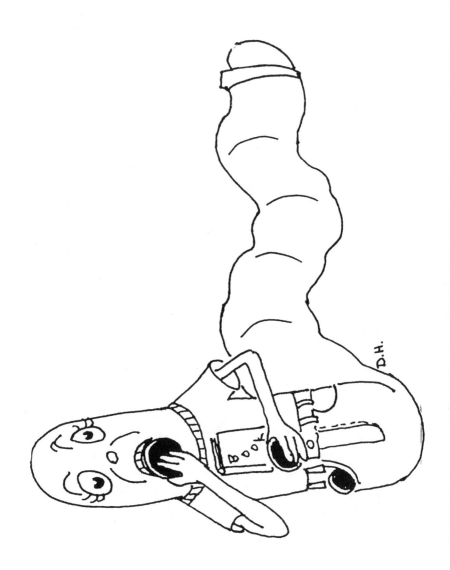

Getting Started (Two groups, 15 minutes)

The Master Bookworms and the Ph.D. Bookworms are in their groups or circles. Give out Bookworm name tags. Tell the children that they are going to make a bookworm book called, "The Missing Oreos." Give the children the three drawings of the Oreo bookworms. Explain these will be the illustrations for their story. Give each child two pieces of cardboard and several sheets of typing paper. Explain that the cardboard will be the covers for their books.

Read the following prompts and let the children write their answers on their paper. (Librarian can help.)

The main character of your book is a bookworm. You need to give the bookworm a name. Write his name under the first bookworm picture. (Bookworm eating Oreos.)

Where does your bookworm live?

Bookworms love Oreos. One day your bookworm's Oreos were missing. When your bookworm couldn't find them, he was very sad. (Hold up a drawing of sad bookworm so they can find their own copy.)

What will your bookworm do to find the Oreos? How did your bookworm solve the mystery?

Now you have a happy bookworm. So you have a happy ending. (Show drawing of happy bookworm.)

Have the children write "The Missing Oreos" at the top of one piece of cardboard, and draw a bookworm underneath. They write their names at the bottom of that piece of cardboard. This will be the front cover for their book.

On the first page they write "The Missing Oreos" and the author's name again. This is the *title page*. Leave the back of that page blank. The next page is number 1. Number all remaining pages, and write "The End" on the last page.

Staple the covers and pages together.

Anyone who does not finish will have time to do so at the end of the day.

Story Time (One group, 15 minutes)

The librarian reads a book about worms. (See the Bookworm Book List.)

Library Time (One group, 15 minutes)

Show a film about worms, books, or hats.

Bookworm Games (One group, 15 minutes)

"The Bookworm Bounce." This is repeated from the first-day program.

"Looby Bookworm." Library bookworms make a circle. They act out the words to the song, sung to the tune of "Looby Loo."

I put my bookworm head in,
I put my bookworm head out,
I give my bookworm head a shake, shake, shake,
And turn myself about.

I put my bookworm tongue in
I put my bookworm tongue out,
I give my bookworm tongue a shake, shake, shake,
And turn myself about.

I wiggle myself in,
I wiggle myself out,
I wiggle myself all over the place,
And turn myself about.

Yes, we are wiggle bookworms,
Yes, we are. (*Wiggle.*)
Yes, we are reading bookworms,
Yes, we are. (*Put two hands together as a book.*)

Yes, I am a library bookworm. (*The children point to themselves.*)
Are you a library bookworm, too? (*They point to someone else.*)

Bookworm Crafts (Two groups, 30 minutes)

Bookworm Big Hats. See pattern, right. Use any color cardboard or poster board. Draw an 8" circle. Cut out the circle. Draw a 5" circle inside the 8" circle (1½ inches from edge of 8" circle). Make a small hole with scissors in the center. Insert scissors into the center and cut toward the inner circle. Start each time from the center of the circle, and cut triangle to the 5" circle line. The small ends of the triangles point into the center of the big circle. Make triangles about

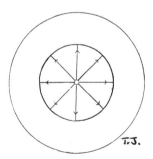

1½" wide at the base. This forms the top of the hat where the child's head goes through.

Try the hat on. If it doesn't fit, cut longer triangles. For a small head, cut shorter triangles.

Washup (One group at a time, 5 minutes)

Snack (One group, 10 minutes)

Oreos and milk. Before snack time, try the following "quiz":

There are Oreo eaters and there are Oreo eaters. Library Bookworms eat their Oreos in the following ways:

1. Bookworms who pull their Oreo apart are called "Splitters."

2. Bookworms who lick off the vanilla frosting inside the Oreo are call "Scrapers."

3. Bookworms who put the chocolate cookie together again are called "Binders."

4. Bookworms who eat the whole Oreo without splitting it, scraping it, or binding it, are called "Bookers."

How do you eat *your* Oreos?

Bookworm Drama (One group, 30 minutes)

Rehearse the play "The Hatters." Be sure the stand-ins rehearse their parts.

Finishing Up (Two groups, 15 minutes)

Finish the story "The Missing Oreos." Collect name tags. Remind the actors to know their lines for the next time.

Tell the children to bring any kind of a hat to the following session. There will be a Hat Fashion Show. Also, tell the children to bring any funny trim to add to their big hats for next time: bows, sequins, small figures, anything that can be glued to the hat.

189

Grades 1–4, Long Program: Third Day

Materials Checklist

____ bookworm name tags (from previous days)
____ hats for "Hat Fashion Show" (children were to bring—have a few on hand for forgetters)
____ real or pretend microphone for "The Hat Fashion Show"
____ record or tape of "fashion-show" music
____ record or tape player
____ markers and/or crayons
____ Big Hats (from previous day)
____ trims to decorate Big Hats
____ Library Bookworm Paper Doll and clothes (from this book)—enough for group
____ white cardboard backing for paper doll (optional)
____ white glue
____ scissors
____ tongue depressors or Popsicle sticks
____ book about hats
____ "Sleuthing Out the Card Catalog" (from this book)
____ paper napkins
____ paper cups
____ veggies
____ dip
____ potato chips
____ V-8 juice
____ scripts for play "The Hatters"
____ props for play (see page 181)

The Program

Goal

To work together in getting ready for a play performance.

Preparation

Photocopy Bookworm Paper Doll and its hats, page 192. Make enough copies for group. Photocopy "Sleuthing Out the Card Catalog" (page 43)— enough for group.

Getting Started   (Two groups, 15 minutes)

Give out bookworm name tags.

Decorate Big Hats (from previous session) with trims brought from home or supplied by librarian.

Story Time   (One group, 15 minutes)

Have the Library Bookworms sit in one large circle with the librarian, who wears a hat. Librarian says: "Today we are having a Hat Fashion Show at game time. Now we will read a book about hats. Can you think of a story about hats?" (See Bookworm Book List.) Read the book, then ask: "How many different kinds of hats can you name?" (Policeman, fireman, sailor, Easter, baseball, funny, bonnet, straw, cowboy, nurse, etc.)

Library Time   (One group, 15 minutes)

Using the directions for "Sleuthing Out the Card Catalog," look up hats in catalog. Find a book about hats. Read your hat book. Talk about the books.

Bookworm Games

Present "A Hat Fashion Show." This fashion show is for game time, not a performance. The children stand in a big circle and face right. Start the music. The children make a complete circle to the right. Then they face the center of the circle. (Music is lowered.)

LIBRARIAN: "Welcome to the "Library Bookworms' Hat Fashion Show." Our first bookworm model is: (first name of child and add "Bookworm." *Example:* Fred Bookworm. "Fred is wearing a red fireman's hat of shiny plastic." Fred models fireman's hat. He walks into center of circle slowly, turns slowly, and walks back to his place in the circle. Each child models his or her hat this way as the librarian describes it.

Bookworm paper doll and hats.

192

When each hat has been described, the bookworms turn to the right and walk around in a circle until they return to their starting place. The music is louder for the circle modeling.

Bookworm Crafts (Two groups, 30 minutes)

Bookworm Paper Doll. Each child receives a photocopy of the bookworm paper doll to color and cut out. Now the children lay the paper dolls on cardboard and trace around them. They cut out the cardboard patterns and then paste the bookworm paper doll drawings to the cardboard pattern. This makes a strong backing for the paper dolls.

The children color the bookworm paper doll's hats and cut them out. Now the bookworm paper dolls can be played with or used as ornaments on a dresser or table, and they make fun gifts.

Remember: Do not cut the tabs on the paper doll clothes. They are needed to fold back to keep the clothes on the paper dolls.

Washup (One group at a time, 5 minutes)

Snack (One group, 10 minutes)

"Bookworm veggies" with "Bookworm dip," potato chips and V-8 juice.

Have one large plate with cut-up vegetables like celery, carrots, small pieces of lettuce, etc.; a basket of potato chips; and a dish with "bookworm dip" (any packaged dip, or mayonnaise and mustard, or horseradish and catsup).

Bookworm Drama (One group, 30 minutes)

Dress rehearsal for the play "The Hatters."

Finishing Up (Two groups, 15 minutes)

Make bookworm stickpuppets from the Bookworm Paper Doll. Glue a tongue depressor or Popsicle stick to the back of the bookworm paper doll.

The stickpuppets model their new hats. They are waved in the air to model, or they can appear at the edge of a table or chair.

Collect bookworm name tags.

Grades 1–4, Long Program: Fourth Day

Materials Checklist

_____ bookworm name tags (from previous days)

_____ small bookworm copied from this book (four small bookworms for each child for mobiles)

_____ markers or crayons

_____ book about hats

_____ typing paper

_____ construction paper or cardboard

_____ stapler

_____ tongue depressors, Popsicle sticks or straws for mobile

_____ heavy thread or fishing line

_____ paper cups

_____ paper napkins

_____ cupcakes

_____ milk

_____ costumes, props, makeup, music, etc. for the play "The Hatters" (see page 181)

_____ copies of "A Bookworm Bookmaking Script" (from this book)

_____ scissors

_____ big bookworm pictures copied from this book, for book cover (one for each child)

_____ varnish (optional)

_____ small brushes, if varnish is used

_____ white glue

_____ paper punch

_____ chairs for Parents' Day audience

_____ A real apple, pencil, and Oreo for children to use as drawing models (optional)

_____ Big Hats (from previous days)

_____ cleansing cream

_____ tissues

The Program

Goal

To make and illustrate a Bookworm Book, and to present play for audience.

Preparation

Photocopy and reduce bookworm on page 176 to use for mobiles; each child will need four small bookworms. Photocopy "A Bookworm Bookmaking Script"—pages 196–197, one for each child. Set up chairs for Parents' Day audience.

Getting Started *and* Library Time (Two groups, 30 minutes)

Give out bookworm name tags. Tell the children they are going to make and illustrate a bookworm book. The book is called "About Bookworms."

Each child receives a copy of "A Bookworm Bookmaking Script" pages 196–197. The children will cut out the paragraphs of the story and paste them at the bottom of each page. They will illustrate each page above the words. The number of pages can be cut, depending on the speed of the child.

It takes one sheet of typing paper to make up each complete book. Fold the paper in half and cut to make 4¼ x 5½ sheets. Now fold each sheet again so the sheets become the pages of the little book. You will have a dedication page and six pages of text and drawings.

Make a cover from cardboard or construction paper, a little larger than the pages.

Explain about dedicating the book to someone special.

Have the children number the pages, cut and paste in the text of the book and draw the pictures that go with the story.

Tell the children: "It is fun to draw Library Bookworms. Think how an angleworm looks, draw it, then put a face, glasses and a hat on it. To illustrate a book is easy to do, and fun, even if you aren't a super artist. Make the drawings your way. The Librarian can help you. Bookworms can be drawn any way, as no two bookworms look alike. It is fun to make a very small bookworm book."

Staple the folded side of the book and cover in three places, top, middle and bottom.

On the cover, children write, "About Bookworms," and "By _____ (name of child)." They draw their own small bookworm for cover illustrations.

Nothing goes inside the front cover. On the next page put to whom you wish to dedicate the book.

Now follow along on your "Bookworm Bookmaking Script."

A Bookworm Bookmaking Script

Page 1.
Bookworms lived about 1,000 years ago in China and Japan. This was when the first books were made.
(Cut out the above-typed words and paste on page 1. Draw a bookworm with Oriental eyes.)

Page 2.
A bookworm is an insect larva (worm) that likes to eat the paste from the binding of a book.
(Cut out the above-typed words and paste on page 2. Draw a bookworm eating the binding of a book. Show the binding, or where the book is put together.)

Page 3.
There are two kinds of bookworms. One is a real worm, and the other is someone who reads and studies a lot.
(Cut out the above-typed words and paste on page 3. Draw two bookworms, one a worm with a funny face, and the other a person with a funny face.)

Page 4.
Our Library Bookworms are smarter than a common worm. Most Library Bookworms wear glasses.
(Cut out the above-typed words and paste to page 4. Draw a bookworm wearing glasses.)

Page 5.
Our Library Bookworms like Oreo cookies. Some bookworms eat too many cookies. Some bookworms are fat, very fat, from eating too many Oreo cookies.
(Cut out the above-typed words and paste to page 5. Draw a very fat bookworm.)

Page 6.
Bookworms live a long time, unless
they get smashed inside a book.
(Cut out the above-typed words and paste to page 6. Draw a bookworm sticking his head out of a book.)

Bookworm Crafts   (Two groups, 30 minutes)

Bookworm Mobiles. Each child receives four bookworms to color. Then, they cut out the bookworms and add construction paper or cardboard for a backing (optional). For an added finish, varnish the bookworms after the bookworm drawing and backing are pasted together (optional).

Cross two tongue depressors, Popsicle sticks, or straws, and glue or bind with heavy thread to hold them in place. These will be the braces from which the Library Bookworms hang. This makes four ends on which to tie bookworms.

Punch a hole at the top of each bookworm. Tie one end of a heavy thread or fishing line (about 8″ long) to each bookworm, inserting the strings through the holes at top of the bookworm drawings. Tie the other ends of each 8″ string to the four crossed ends of the braces.

Make a hole with an awl or ice pick in the top of the brace where the sticks cross. Now insert a hook (e.g. a cup hook) into the hole, and turn to tighten. String and another hook can be added at home to hang up the bookworm mobile.

Washup   (One group at a time, 5 minutes)

Snack   (Two groups, 10 minutes)

Cupcakes and milk.

Drama   (One group, 30 minutes)

Bookworms return to their circles to get ready for the play "The Hatters." Makeup: Put large, red lipstick circles on bookworms' cheeks. Make big, round glasses on bookworms' faces with eyebrow pencil. Library bookworms put on their big hats they made in crafts.

Present the play "The Hatters" for the audience.

Finishing Up   (Two groups, 15 minutes)

Finish small books, "About Bookworms."

Tell the children what wonderful Library Bookworms they have been. Ask what they liked the best during the Library Bookworm Program.

Take home name tags, crafts, etc. (Some children will want to take off the makeup before they leave, and some won't. Have cleansing cream and tissues on hand.)

Library Bookworms:
Grades 1–4, Short Program
Time: 2 days; 1 1/2 hours each day

Getting Started: Bookworm name tags (10 min.)
Story Time: Book about worms or hats (10 min.)
Library Time: Library tour (10 min.)
Bookworm Games: "Library Stacks Are Falling Down" (5 min.)
Bookworm Crafts: Bookworm Bracelets (15 min.)
Washup and Snack: Applesauce and graham crackers (15 min.)
Bookworm Drama: "The Wiggly Bookworms"—read-through and practice (20 min.)
Finishing Up: Bookworm Paper Doll (5 min.)

SECOND DAY
Getting Started: Choose book(s) for Story Time (10 min.)
Story Time: Read chosen book(s) (10 min.)
Library Time: Film about worms *or* Card Catalog Game (10 min.)
Bookworm Games: "Hide and Seek the Bookworms" (5 min.)
Bookworm Crafts: Bookworm Hand Puppets (15 min.)
Washup and Snack: Cupcakes and lemonade (15 min.)
Bookworm Drama: Present "The Wiggly Bookworms" (20 min.)
Finishing Up (5 min.)

Grades 1–4, Short Program: First Day

Materials Checklist

____ bookworm paper dolls and hats (from this book)
____ bookworm name tags (from this book)
____ yarn for bookworm name tags
____ book for Story Time
____ small bookworm (from this book) for bookworm bracelets
____ cardboard for bookworm backing
____ thin elastic for bookworm bracelets
____ scissors
____ varnish
____ brushes
____ record, tape, or piano music for "The Wiggly Bookworms" play
____ record or tape player
____ white glue
____ markers or crayons
____ paper napkins
____ paper cups
____ plastic spoons
____ applesauce
____ graham crackers
____ envelopes—one for each child
____ copies of the play "The Wiggly Bookworms" (from this book)

The Program

Goal

To think about the library and books.

Preparation

Make one photocopy for each child of the following illustrations: Bookworm name tag, page 176; small bookworm for bracelet, page 176; bookworm paper doll and hats, pages 192. Make four copies of "The Wiggly Bookworms" script, pages 203–204.

Getting Started (Two groups,* 10 minutes)

Make Bookworm name tags, page 176.

Story Time (One group, 10 minutes)

The children sit around the librarian, who reads them a book about worms or hats. (See Bookworm Book List.)

Library Time (Two groups, 10 minutes)

Take a short tour of the library. Point out things the children would find interesting.

A book is read to one group while the other is touring. Talk about the things they saw on return. Who can remember the most?

Bookworm Games (One group, 5 minutes)

"Library Stacks Are Falling Down." Two children make an arch with their hands (as in "London Bridge"). The other children line up in a straight line. The Bookworms sing as they pass under the "book stacks," which are the children's arms.

"The library book stacks are falling down,
Falling down,
Falling down,
The library book stacks are falling down,
What bookworm will they land on?"

The two children whose arms are the book stacks catch the bookworm under them.

The song is repeated until there is only one bookworm left.

Bookworm Crafts (Two groups, 15 minutes)

Bookworm Bracelets. Color the small bookworm that has been photocopied from this book. Cut out the bookworm and glue to a cardboard

*"Two groups" notation signifies that division of a large group is appropriate or desirable for an activity. You may prefer not to divide smaller groups.

backing. Punch holes on either side at the middle of the bookworm's body. Push thin elastic through the two holes and make a knot in one end of the elastic so it will not come through the hole. Measure the elastic so it will go around the child's arm. Tie a knot in the other end. The children slip their hands through the elastic and the bookworm rides on the top of the arm as a bracelet. If the bookworms are varnished, they will last longer and look more like real bracelets.

Washup (One group at a time, 5 minutes)

Snack (One group, 10 minutes)

Applesauce and graham crackers. Put the applesauce in small paper cups.

Drama (One group, 20 minutes)

Read through the play "The Wiggly Bookworms."
Choose the actors.
Rehearse the play for as long as there is time.

Finishing Up (Two groups, 5 minutes)

Color and cut out the bookworm paper doll. Glue to a cardboard backing. Cut out the bookworm hats (no backing). Give each child an envelope to take his or her bookworm paper doll home.

Tell the children to bring a sock next time to make bookworm puppets. (Knee socks are the best. Any color.) Also, bring a man's T-shirt or a woman's large size T-shirt. The T-shirt will be the costume for the play.

Tell the children about Parents' Day. Tell them to ask a friend to come to see the play, or to join the other bookworms for the last program.

Be sure to tell the parents about Parents' Day and tell them to bring a camera for the play, if they wish.

The Wiggly Bookworms
by
Taffy Jones

Characters:

BOOKY BOOKWORM — A shy bookworm
BOOKWORM ONE — A wiggler
BOOKWORM TWO — Another wiggler
OTHER BOOKWORMS
LIBRARIAN
PARENTS

The children learn this play by repetition. Choose an outgoing child for Booky Bookworm. Have another child be an understudy for Booky. Explain to the children what an understudy is. (Someone who takes the place of an actor if he cannot make the performance or show.)

The children wear a man's or woman's large-size T-shirt. Colored strips of material or crepe paper is wrapped around each child's body and T-shirt. Pin the top and bottom of the crepe paper with large safety pins. Remember that crepe paper stretches; some tightening up may be necessary before performance. And remember that crepe paper *runs* — water and crepe paper do not mix!

Put red circles (lipstick) on each child's cheeks. Add black circles (glasses) around their eyes. Add red lips (lipstick). Some will object, especially the boys. Explain that actors wear makeup for plays. If they still object, don't push it. The children bookworms are seated on the floor in front of a line of chairs for the audience. Put on a lively record or tape for some wiggling music. One by one the bookworms jump up and start to dance. They spread out and keep wiggling. After a short time of wiggling, send in Booky Bookworm. Booky does not want to wiggle. Push Booky Bookworm into the dancing even more and leave him/her there.

Booky Bookworm stands still with head down, as the other bookworms wiggle. (Music is lowered.)

BOOKWORM ONE:	(*Wiggles up to Booky.*) Come on, Booky! Get wiggling! (*Wiggles away.*)
BOOKY:	(*Shakes head no, and doesn't move*)

203

OTHER BOOKWORMS:	(*Wiggle closer to Booky.* Come on, Booky Bookworm. Get wiggling!
BOOKWORM TWO:	(*Wiggles to Booky.*) Aw, come on, Booky Bookworm. WIGGLE!
BOOKY:	I don't know how to wiggle.
BOOKWORM ONE:	I'll show you.
BOOKY:	I can never learn.
BOOKWORM ONE:	Sure you can, Booky, Every bookworm knows how to wiggle.
BOOKY:	I don't.
BOOKWORM TWO:	Just wiggle your little finger. You've got to start somewhere.
BOOKY:	(*Wiggles little finger.*)
BOOKWORM ONE:	That's right, Booky. Now wiggle your hand.
BOOKY:	(*Booky wiggles hand.*)
BOOKWORM TWO:	You've got it. Now wiggle your leg.
BOOKY:	(*Booky wiggles leg.*)
BOOKWORM ONE:	Now wiggle all over.
BOOKY:	(*Wiggles all over.*)
BOOKWORMS:	Look at Booky Bookworm wiggle!
BOOKY:	(*Wiggles.*) Look! I'm wiggling. Look, Mom [or Dad, or friend], I'm wiggling. I am a wiggly bookworm. (*Wiggles some more.*) (*Booky wiggles to his parent.*) Wiggle with me. (*The parent, or whoever is chosen, gets up and wiggles with Booky. It is, however, a surprise to this person.*)
BOOKWORMS:	(*Dance and wiggle. Then they shout.*) WIGGLE! (*They dance and wiggle again and shout.*) WIGGLE! (*Once more they dance and shout.*) WIGGLE!! WIGGLE!! (*They go and choose a partner from the audience to wiggle with them. Everyone becomes a Wiggly Library Bookworm.*)

The End

Grades 1–4, Short Program: Second Day

Materials Checklist

____ bookworm name tags (from previous day)
____ books on worms and hats
____ film about worms
____ big and small bookworm (from this book)
____ socks to make bookworm puppets (children were to bring from home, but have some on hand for forgetters)
____ yarn
____ red, pink, or orange felt
____ roly-poly eyes
____ scissors that can cut cloth
____ white glue
____ large safety pins
____ cardboard
____ record, tape or piano for play, "The Wiggly Bookworm"
____ record or tape player
____ red lipstick, black eyebrow pencil for bookworm makeup
____ cleansing cream
____ tissues
____ mirror
____ chairs for Parents' Day audience
____ cupcakes
____ lemonade
____ paper cups
____ paper napkins
____ large T-shirts (children were to bring from home, but have a few on hand)
____ rolls of crepe paper (any color) or strips of material
____ scripts for play "The Wiggly Bookworm" (for teachers)

The Program

Goal

To learn that the library is a fun place to be.

Preparation

Photocopy the bookworm, page 176. Enlarge it by hand or on copier and copy again, so that you have a big and a small bookworm. Hide them somewhere in the library.

Getting Started   (Two groups, 10 minutes)

Give out bookworm name tags.

Children look at books about worms and hats that the librarian has pulled from the shelves. They talk about the different kinds of hats bookworms could *wear*: policeman's, fireman's, cowboy, nurse's, baseball, etc. They choose a book for Story Time.

Story Time   (One group, 10 minutes)

Read one or two of the books the children have chosen during "Getting Started."

Library Time   (One group, 10 minutes)

Show a film about worms. If this is not possible, play the "Card Catalog Game": Have the children sit on the floor around the Card Catalog. Tell the children you are going to look for the word "Worms" in the Card Catalog. Show them how to look for the letter "W" on the front of the drawers. Show them how to look up the subjects of worms.

Find a book about worms listed in the Card Catalog. Read what it says on the card. Put the drawer back in the stand. Now ask one of the children to see if they could find the book in the Card Catalog. (Help if necessary.)

Have the children say the alphabet together and clap their hands on each letter, in between looking up books on worms in the Card Catalog.

Bookworm Games   (One group, 10 minutes)

"Hide and Seek the Bookworms." Tell the children that in a given area there are a small bookworm and a large bookworm hiding (see "Preparation"). See who can find them. The ones who find the bookworms get to keep them.

If the bookworms are found quickly, have the children who find the bookworms hide them. This game can be repeated as many times as desired. The first finders keep the bookworms.

Bookworm Crafts   (Two groups, 15 minutes)

Bookworm Hand Puppets. Take a sock and cut across the top, where the toes go, to make the mouth opening. You need to stick the point of the scissors through the top of the sock to get started.

Next, cut cardboard to fit the mouth opening and fold the cardboard in half. Cut out an oval liner of red, orange or pink felt, slightly larger than the cardboard (enough that it can be glued over the sides of the cardboard oval); set aside.

Glue the edges of the sock at the mouth opening around the folded cardboard mouth. Be sure all the edges are glued down. Hold you fingers on the sock until you know it is sticking. (Takes a couple of minutes.)

Now glue the felt mouth liner over the cardboard, covering the glued sock edges. Close the bookworm's mouth and hold it tight to press the glue. Now the bookworm has a mouth that opens. Cut a felt tongue and glue it in the bookworm's mouth.

For hair, take strands of yarn, all the same length, and tie them in the middle. Braids can be made, or long hair, etc. Pin the hair to the top of the sock with a large safety pin.

Glue on roly-poly eyes. Here again, pressure must be applied after gluing. Use plenty of glue and wipe away the excess.

The puppeteers slide their hands into the opening of the sock and fit their hands around the cardboard mouth. Now they can open and close the bookworm's mouth. Bookworm puppets do a lot of talking.

Washup   (One group at a time, 5 minutes)

Snack   (One group, 10 minutes)

Cupcakes and lemonade.

Drama   (One group, 15 minutes)

Put on the bookworms' costumes and makeup. The parents can help. Present the play "The Wiggly Bookworms." (Note: If not enough time for the play, cut Story Time.)

Boy with Bookworm Hand Puppets.

Finishing Up   (Two groups, 10 minutes)

Tell the children what great wiggle bookworms they were. Take makeup off the children who do not want to wear it home. Be sure the children take home their bookworm puppets, bookworm name tags, etc.

Tell the children always to be a reading bookworm and visit the library often. It is a fun place to be.

Library Bookworms
Preschool–Kindergarten, Long Program
Time: 2 days; 1 1/2 hours each day

FIRST DAY

Getting Started: Bookworm name tags and roll call (10 min.)
Story Time: Book about worms (10 min.)
Library Time: Library tour (10 min.)
Bookworm Games: "The Bookworm Wiggle" (5 min.)
Bookworm Crafts: Wiggly Pipe Cleaner Bookmarks (15 min.)
Washup and Snack: Apple slices and apple juice (15 min.)
Bookworm Drama: "The Wiggly Bookworms"—read-through (20 min.)
Finishing Up (5 min.)

SECOND DAY

Getting Started: Frost bookworm Twinkies (10 min.)
Story Time: Book about worms (10 min.)
Library Time: Film about worms (10 min.)
Bookworm Games: "Bookworm Says" (5 min.)
Bookworm Crafts: Jumping Bookworms (15 min.)
Washup and Snack: Bookworm Twinkies, grape juice (15 min.)
Bookworm Drama: Present "The Wiggly Bookworms" (20 min.)
Finishing Up (5 min.)

Preschool–Kindergarten Long Program:
First Day

Materials Checklist

____ bookworm name tags (from this book)
____ yarn for name tags
____ white glue
____ pipe cleaners
____ paper punch
____ markers (mostly black and red)
____ cardboard for name tag backing (optional)
____ 1½" x 1" cardboard for bookworm eyes
____ fiction and non-fiction books about worms
____ lively record or tape for "The Bookworm Wiggle" game
____ apples
____ apple juice
____ paper cups
____ paper napkins
____ bookworm paper doll and hats (from this book)—enough copies for group
____ two copies of play "The Wiggly Bookworm" (from this book)
____ men's T-shirt (no artwork)
____ roll of crepe paper or strips of material
____ safety pins

The Program

Goals

To interact with other children and learn self expression; to learn about fiction and non-fiction books.

Preparation

Photocopy the bookworm name tag, page 176, and the bookworm paper doll and hats, pages 192—enough for each child to have a copy of everything. Make two copies of "The Wiggly Bookworm," pages 203–204, for the librarian and an assistant. Slice up apples for snack time.

Getting Started   (Two groups,* 10 minutes)

The children are divided into two bookworm groups or circles at opposite ends of the room. Preschoolers are the Squirmy Worms and the kindergarteners are the Wiggly Worms.

The bookworm name tags are given out. For this age group you may wish to do much of the preparation yourself ahead of time.

Now do a *Bookworm Roll Call*: Each child says his or her first name and adds "Bookworm" for the last name. (*Example:* "I am Ellen Bookworm." "I am Scott Bookworm.") Each bookworm should stand as he or she speaks. This gives the children the experience of speaking in front of others. Be sure each bookworm speaks clearly and loudly enough to be heard. Have them say their name over, if necessary.

Story Time   (One group, 10 minutes)

The two bookworm groups join together for Story Time. They sit on the floor around the librarian's chair. The librarian reads them a fiction book about worms. (See the Bookworm Book List.) There is a discussion about the difference between worms and bookworms. Sample questions: Did you ever see a worm? Where? Do you like worms? Do you think a worm is pretty? Are you afraid of a worm? Did you ever go fishing and use a worm for bait? Did you put the worm on the hook? Are there good and bad worms? Can you name one good worm? (Earthworm, who enriches the soil.) Can you name one bad worm? (Tent caterpillar, who eats the leaves on the trees.) Did you ever hear of a bookworm? Do you think there are real bookworms? There are two kinds of bookworms: The real worm, who eats the paste from books, and the human kind, who reads a lot of books.

---

*"Two groups" notation signifies that division of a large group is appropriate or desirable for an activity. You may prefer not to divide smaller groups.

Library Bookworms

Read a book about real worms. Get the facts on the worms. (See Bookworm Book List.)

The librarian says, "That was a story about real worms. When a story is about real things and tell information, the book is a non-fiction book. Now say *non-fiction*. Say after me. *Non-fiction*." (*Children reply.*)

"If a story is make-believe, it is called a fiction book. Now say after me. Fiction." (*Children reply.*)

"Now say fiction and non-fiction." (*Repeat and say the words faster and faster. Clap hands.*)

Library Time   (Two groups, 10 minutes)

Take a tour of the library. An assistant reads a fiction book about worms to one group while the other group is touring.

Bookworm Games   (One group, 5 minutes)

"The Bookworm Wiggle Game." Put on a lively or popular record or tape for wiggling music. The children, standing in a circle, wiggle as long as the music is playing. Pick up the needle, or stop the tape. When the music stops, the children hold a bookworm pose while the librarian tries to make them laugh, talk or move. If they do any of these things, they are "out." This is repeated as long as you wish. Between the bookworm poses, the children can rest by curling up like a bookworm on the floor.

Bookworm Crafts   (Two groups, 15 minutes)

Wiggly Pipe Cleaner Bookworms. Give each child a pipe cleaner and a small piece of any colored cardboard, about one and one-half inches long by one inch wide, and a piece of another pipe cleaner about two inches long, for the glasses. They will use a black magic marker to mark the eyes on the cardboard. They cut the eyes from the cardboard and glue the glasses around the eyes.

Washup   (One group at a time, 5 minutes)

The Squirmy Worms go first for washup while the Wiggly Worms start coloring the bookworm paper dolls that have been photocopied from this book. The Wiggly Worms follow for washup when the Squirmy Worms have finished. Then the Squirmy Worms start their snacks, later joined by the Wiggly Worms.

Snack   (One group, 10 minutes)

Cut-up apples and apple juice would be good for snacks. Count on two apple slices per child and one paper cup of fruit juice. Then add a few more for extras and the number of helpers.

Bookworm Drama   (One Group, 15 minutes)

Read through the play "The Wiggly Bookworm." The children should be in one group for the reading.

Choose the lead actors with care. Choose children who are outgoing and can speak out. Tell about the bookworm costumes and makeup all the bookworms will wear. Use one child as a model; have him or her put on the white T-shirt you have brought, and show others how crepe paper will be wrapped around them to make them into bookworms. Also tell how the makeup will be: circles of lipstick on the cheeks, and "glasses" made with black eyebrow pencil.

Ask the children to wear large men's or women's T-shirts (preferably with no art work) to the next session of the program, over their regular clothes.

Now, go through the play, "The Wiggly Bookworms," with Booky Bookworm acting out the part along with the other bookworms. Encourage the children to be free and alive and have fun being wiggly bookworms. Excite the children about the surprise ending of having their parents or friend come up and wiggle with them. Tell the children this is a secret. Can they keep a secret? It's more fun if they do.

Finishing Up   (Two groups, 5 minutes)

The children go back to their groups, the Wiggly Worms and the Squirmy Worms. Finish bookworm paper dolls. Collect name tags.

Tell the parents about "Parents' Day," the next session of the program. Tell them to bring a camera if they wish. Tell the children to bring a friend to wiggle with them next time. Explain to the parents about the T-shirts.

Preschool–Kindergarten, Long Program: Second Day

Materials Checklist

___ bookworm name tags (from previous day)
___ trays or cardboard covered with aluminum foil for bookworm Twinkies
___ aluminum foil or wax paper
___ plastic knives, or knives made of white cardboard
___ one Twinkie for each child
___ two chocolate chips for each child
___ two gumdrops for each child
___ two toothpicks for each child
___ a can of frosting (any flavor)
___ two bowls for frosting (plastic or paper)
___ two paper plates for gumdrops
___ grape juice
___ paper napkins
___ paper cups
___ a picture book for each child
___ 4" of chenille doll hair for each child
___ half a pipe cleaner for each child
___ 8" of thin, elastic thread for each child
___ two roly-poly eyes for each child
___ paper towels
___ chairs for Parents' Day audience
___ white glue
___ film about worms
___ scissors
___ paper punch
___ cleansing cream
___ tissues
___ makeup for play (lipstick, eyebrow pencil)
___ large white T-shirts (children were to bring, but have extras on hand)
___ rolls of crepe paper
___ safety pins

The Program

Goal

To present play for audience.

Preparation

Set up chairs for Parents' Day audience.

Getting Started   (Two groups, 10 minutes)

Give out the bookworm name tags. Have the children quickly wash their hands. Have in front of each child a Twinkie on a piece of aluminum foil or wax paper (about a 10″ piece). Give each child a small plastic knife, or cut small knives from cardboard. Place two bowls of frosting (any flavor, taken from ready-made frosting cans) at the ends of the table.

Tell the children they are frosting bookworm Twinkies for Snack Time. The bowls are passed to the children so they can each take a scoop of frosting. The bowls keep going around until each child has frosted a Twinkie. This way, each child has a fair chance of frosting a Twinkie and it makes it a game.

When the Twinkies are frosted, bring out two paper plates with chocolate chips on them. These are passed around the table, with each child taking two chocolate chips. These are for the bookworm eyes.

Next, give each child two toothpicks. They stick these on the head of the bookworm Twinkies. They are the feelers.

Now put two plates on the table with small gumdrops. The gumdrops are pushed onto the toothpicks. These are the tops of the feelers.

Have the children then put their bookworm Twinkies on a tray (or cardboard) covered with aluminum foil. Have the bookworm Twinkies lined up one after the other, if there is room on the tray, or winding around like one big bookworm.

Pass around a wet paper towel to clean their hands. Then pass around dry paper towels.

Story Time   (One group, 10 minutes)

Book about worms. (See Bookworm Book List.)

Library Time   (One group, 10 minutes)

Show a film about worms.

Bookworm Games   (One group, 5 minutes)

"Bookworm Says." Have the children stand around the librarian. Play the game, "Bookworm Says." It is played like "Simon Says." The librarian gives each child a picture book. The children are to do as she says, except when she doesn't say, "Bookworm Says."

Bookworm says—"Open your book."
Bookworm says—"Close your book."
Bookworm says—"Open your book."
Bookworm says—"Read your book."
Now turn the page.

Bookworm says—"Turn a page."
Bookworm says—"Turn another page."
Now turn another page.

Bookworm says—"Hold up your book."
Let us see the book.
Put the book down.

Bookworm says—"Stand up."
Bookworm says—"Sit down."
Bookworm says—"Stand up."
Bookworm says—"Sit down."
Stand up.
Now please give me your books. ("I didn't say, 'Bookworm says,' I was polite, however.")
See how many winners there are. Those who didn't do what bookworm says each time are out.

Bookworm Crafts   (Two groups, 15 minutes)

Jumping Bookworms. Each child has about 4" of chenille doll hair (buy at any craft shop, Woolworth's, or other places that have craft supplies), half a pipe cleaner, about 8" of thin, elastic thread and two roly-poly eyes. Glasses for the bookworms are made from the pipe cleaner. The chenille doll hair is the bookworm's body. Tie the elastic thread around the furry bookworm's neck with one end and make a small loop at the other end for the finger to go through.

Now the children can make their bookworm jump up and down. They give their bookworm a name and make them jump during the play, "The Wiggly Bookworms."

Washup   (One group at a time, 5 minutes)

Snack   (One group, 10 minutes)

Bookworm Twinkies and grape juice.

Drama   (One group, 20 minutes)

Present the play, "The Wiggly Bookworm." Parents or assistants help with costumes and makeup. Children take their Jumping Bookworms for the play and wiggle them up and down. Have picture-taking time afterwards.

Finishing Up   (Two groups, 5 minutes)

Talk about the things the children did in the Bookworm Program. Tell the children they were great Squirmy and Wiggly Worms. Have them check out a book to take home, along with their bookworm name tags, crafts, costumes, etc.

Remove makeup from the bookworms who do not wish to wear their makeup home.

Tell the children to come back soon.

Library Bookworms:
Preschool–Kindergarten, Short Program
Time: One day; 1 1/2 hours

Getting Started: Bookworm name tags; talk about worms (10 min.)
Story Time: Book about worms (10 min.)
Library Time: Library tour (10 min.)
Bookworm Games: "Follow the Bookworm" (5 min.)
Bookworm Crafts: Bookworm and Bookworm Carrying Case (15 min.)
Washup and Snack: Popcorn and fruit juice (15 min.)
Bookworm Drama: "The Wiggly Bookworms" (20 min.)
Finishing Up (5 min.)

Materials Checklist

_____ bookworm name tags (from this book)
_____ cardboard for name tag backing (optional)
_____ yarn for name tags and carrying case
_____ typing paper
_____ white glue
_____ paper punch
_____ small and big bookworms (from this book)
_____ crayons or markers
_____ book about worms
_____ record or tape of lively music
_____ record or tape player
_____ popcorn in baggies
_____ fruit juice
_____ paper cups
_____ lipstick and black eyebrow pencil
_____ tissues
_____ cleansing cream
_____ chairs for audience
_____ two copies of "The Wiggly Bookworms" (from this book)

The Program

Goals

To see that the library is a fun and friendly place to be; to know that smart bookworms go to the library.

218

Preparation

Photocopy bookworm name tag, page 176—enough copies for group. Also reduce the drawing to make one small bookworm for each child; then enlarge that picture and copy one *big* bookworm for each child. Make two copies of "The Wiggly Bookworms," pages 203–204—one for librarian and one for an assistant.

Getting Started   (Two groups,* 10 minutes)

The children are divided into bookworm groups or circles at opposite ends of the room. Preschoolers are the Squirmy Worms and the kindergarteners are the Wiggly Worms.

Give out name tags. Also give out crayons, markers, and typing paper for drawing.

Talk about worms. Ask: Have you ever seen a worm? Where did you see the worm? Are there good worms? (Earthworms enrich the soil.) Are there bad worms? (Tent caterpillar eat the leaves of the trees.) Are you afraid of a worm? Draw on the paper in front of you what you think a worm looks like.

Did you ever hear of a bookworm? Yes? No? There is a worm that likes to get inside a book and eat the paste that holds the book together. It's called a bookworm.

There is another kind of bookworm: a person who studies and reads a lot. Being a Library Bookworm is fun. Let's read a story about a worm and we will be smart Library Bookworms.

Story Time   (One group, 10 minutes)

The two bookworm groups join together for Story Time. The librarian reads them a book about worms. (See Bookworm Book List.)

Library Time   (Two groups, 10 minutes)

One group tours as the other group has a book about worms read to them.

*"Two groups" notation signifies that division of a large group is appropriate or desirable for an activity. You may prefer not to divide smaller groups.

Bookworm Games (One group, 5 minutes)

"Follow the Bookworm." The children line up. The leader moves around the room doing different actions such as clapping, wiggling, jumping, skipping, etc. The other children imitate the actions. After the leader has done a few actions, he or she goes to the end of the line, and the next bookworm becomes the leader.

Bookworm Crafts (Two groups, 15 minutes)

Bookworm and a Bookworm Carrying Case. Have the children color the big bookworm and the small bookworm. Turn down the top of the small bookworm drawing (it should be photocopied on 8½ x 11" paper) about 2". This is the front of the carrying case.

Now punch two holes in a piece of typing paper, one on the right and one on the left, each about 1" from the top and side. Thread any color yarn, about 26" long, from the right hole to the left hole. Tie the two ends together. This becomes the handle for the carrying case.

Paste the two sides and bottom of the carrying case together.

Cut out the big bookworm and put it in the carrying case. If you make a cardboard backing for the big bookworm, it will be stronger.

Now you have a big bookworm in a bookworm carrying case.

Washup (One group at a time, 5 minutes)

Snack (One group, 10 minutes)

Popcorn and fruit juice.

Drama (One group, 20 minutes)

Do "The Wiggly Bookworms." When you feel the children have a handle on the play, ask the parents to come in to see it.

Finishing Up (Two groups, 5 minutes)

Tell the little bookworms how great they have been. You are proud of them because they are now true Library Bookworms. Tell them to come to the library and take home books. Remind them the library is a special place. When you read a book, it is like wearing magic glasses.

5. Library Indians

Learning about the American Indians is the focus of the Library Indians programs. The history of the native American tribes is taught through reading, discussion, and drama. Craft activities reinforce learning about native artwork.

Other goals of the Library Indians include getting to know the library, and writing and performing original plays.

Library Indians:
Grades 1–4, Long Program
Time: 4 days; 2 1/2 hours each day

FIRST DAY
Getting Started: Indian name tags, Parents' Day invitations (15 min.)
Story Time: Book about American Indians (15 min.)
Library Talk: Talk about American Indians; library tour (15 min.)
Indian Games: "Sharp Indian Eyes" (15 min.)
Indian Crafts: Indian Headbands (30 min.)
Washup and Snack: Popcorn and apple juice (15 min.)
Indian Drama: "Bookeyes and Library Hawks"—read-through (30 min.)
Finishing Up (15 min.)

SECOND DAY
Getting Started: Color Indian designs (15 min.)
Story Time: Book about American Indians (15 min.)
Library Time: Film about Indians (15 min.)
Indian Games: "Ten Little Indians" (15 min.)
Indian Crafts: Tomahawks (30 min.)
Washup and Snack: Animal crackers and milk (15 min.)
Indian Drama: "Bookeyes and Library Hawks"—practice (30 min.)
Finishing Up (15 min.)

THIRD DAY
Getting Started: Color Indian masks (15 min.)
Story Time: Books about American Indian arts and crafts (15 min.)
Library Time: Indian clay pots (15 min.)
Indian Games: "Who's Chief?" (15 min.)
Indian Crafts: Indian shields (30 min.)
Washup and Snack: Veggies, corn chips, V-8 (15 min.)
Indian Drama: "Bookeyes and Library Hawks"—dress rehearsal (30 min.)
Finishing Up: Indian Makeup (15 min.)

FOURTH DAY
Getting Started: Talk about writing plays (15 min.)
Story Time: Read a play (15 min.)
Library Time: Write a play about American Indians (15 min.)
Indian Crafts: Library Indian Paper Dolls (30 min.)
Washup and Snack: Corn muffins or cupcakes, fruit drink (15 min.)
Indian Drama: Present "Bookeyes and Library Hawks" (30 min.)
Finishing Up (15 min.)

Grades 1–4, Long Program: First Day

Materials Checklist

____ Indian shield name tags (from this book)—two for each child, plus a
few extra
____ crayons and markers (especially red and blue)
____ white cardboard for name tag backing (optional)
____ red and blue yarn for name tags
____ scissors
____ white glue
____ Indian book selections
____ construction paper
____ red and blue feathers (optional)
____ stapler
____ paper punch
____ popcorn
____ apple juice
____ paper napkins
____ paper cups
____ seven copies of script for play, "Bookeyes and Library Hawks" (from
this book)
____ props for play (see page 227)—note that some props will be made
during craft time on later days of program (eg. tomahawks)

The Program

Goals

To learn about fiction and non-fiction books, and to think about the
American Indians.

Preparation

Enlarge (by hand or on copier) the Indian name tags on page 224. (You
can use them actual size if you prefer.) Make enough copies for each child
to have two—one for name tag, one to use for Parent's Day invitation. You
may wish to further prepare name tags for Grades 1–2 (see "Getting Started").

Make seven photocopies of the play, "Bookeyes and Library Hawks" (pages 227–231).

Getting Started   (Two groups,* 15 minutes)

The children are seated in two "Indian Circles." Grades 1–2 are the Bookeyes, with red colors, and Grades 3–4 are the Library Hawks, with blue. The children color their name tags and write their names on the tags. White cardboard backing for the name tags will make them stronger (optional). Punch a hole at the top of the shield for the yarn to go through— red or blue yarn, depending on the tribe's color. The yarn ties around the neck of the child.

Bookeyes color the Bookeyes shield and the Library Hawks color the Library Hawks shield for the Parents' Day Invitations. Cut out and write on the white side of the shield the place, date, and time.

Story Time   (One group, 15 minutes)

Read a story about American Indians. (See Indian Book List.)

Library Time   (One group, 15 minutes)

Talk about American Indians. Do you know any American Indians? Where do some of the Indians live? Do you think the white people treated the Indians fairly? Do they treat them well now? Are you proud of the Indians? Why?

Who discovered America? When? What were the Indians like then? And now? Were the Indians friendly to the white settlers? And now?

Look over other books about American Indians. (See Book List.) Take a tour of the library. While one group is touring, the other group talks about the Indians and has another book read to them.

Indian Games   (One group, 15 minutes)

"Sharp Indian Eyes." American Indians could spot a deer in the deep woods or find wild berries in a field, because they learned to use their eyes

*Two groups" notation signifies that division of a large group is appropriate or desirable for an activity. You may prefer not to divide small groups.

Opposite: Library Hawk (top) and Bookeye name tags.

and observe carefully. Library Indians can see many things in their library and can spot any kind of book. How many things can you see from where you are sitting in the library? You may see something as small as a pencil or as large as a book stack. How about the clock? Time this game (1 or 2 minutes). Children can take turns calling out what they see. The child who tells the most things in the shortest time is the winner.

Indian Crafts   (Two groups, 30 minutes)

Indian Headbands. Measure a child's head around the forehead. Cut a strip of white construction paper slightly longer then the head measurement and about 1½ inches wide. The children draw Indian designs on these with red or blue crayons or markers. Staple the ends together. Staple a red or blue feather to the back of each band. Feathers are easily found in craft shops or discount department stores, or you can make paper feathers from construction paper or thin cardboard. Shape the feather from the paper. Draw a line down the middle of the feather. Then cut lines from the outside in, to make the feather look feathery. The black lines make the feather look real. The children write their names on the headbands. They make up Indian names for themselves. *Examples*: Running Bear, Flying Eagle, Running Deer.

Washup   (One group at a time, 5 minutes)

Library Hawks follow Bookeyes.

Snack   (One group, 10 minutes)

Place a handful of popcorn in a paper napkin and tie. Serve with apple juice. The American Indians like corn and apples.

Indian Drama   (One group, 30 minutes)

Read through the play "Bookeyes and Library Hawks." Choose characters and check props. Start rehearsing the play.

Finishing Up   (Two groups, 15 minutes)

Play characters take home scripts to learn. (Note: If you feel there will not be enough time to learn lines, the librarian can read the story as the children act it out.)

Take home Parents' Day invitations. Make extra invitations to take to friends.

Collect name tags.

226

Bookeyes and Library Hawks

A Library Play
by
Taffy Jones

Characters:

NARRATOR (Librarian or one of the children)
CHIEF BOOKEYE
CHIEF HAWKEYE
LIBRARY HAWKS
HARRIED PARENT
PROFESSOR
LIBRARIAN
BOOKEYES and LIBRARY HAWKS (all other children, in two groups)

Props:

Indian headbands, Indian make-up, Indian jewelry
tomahawks and shields
drum
book for Professor
shopping bag and baby carriage for Parent (optional)
Book of Peace (book with "PEACE" taped over title)
pretend microphone (roll from paper towels)

NARR.	Hello, I am _____, librarian of the _____ Library. I have a story to tell you. I think you will like it.
	Once upon a time, there lived in the _____ Library, two Indian tribes—the Bookeyes and the Library Hawks. These two library tribes got along very well until one day, when the Bookeyes decided that fiction books were the best. The Library Hawks heard them talking and immediately declared that non-fiction books were best.

227

Library Indians

TRIBES:	*(The Bookeyes are lined up on one side of the room and the Library Hawks are lined up on the other side. The Bookeyes talk together and then yell, "Fiction!" The Library Hawks talk together and then yell, "Non-Fiction!")*
NARR.:	It became a very bad situation in the library.
TRIBES:	*(They walk toward each other, the Bookeyes passing in back of the Library Hawks, their arms folded across their chests.)*
NARR.:	At first, the two tribes wouldn't talk to one another.
TRIBES:	*(They go to opposite sides of the room, then turn to go back the way they came.)*
NARR.:	Later, the Bookeyes and the Library Hawks yelled and screamed at each other whenever they met.
TRIBES:	*(Bookeyes yell "Fiction," and the Library Hawks yell, "Non-Fiction," as they pass each other going to the other side of the room.)*
NARR.:	It wasn't long before the two tribes were enemies. Whenever the two tribes met, they started shoving each other around.
TRIBES:	*(Shove one another as they proceed to the other side again.)*
NARR.:	At last, sad to say, the Bookeyes and the Library Hawks were on the warpath. They picked up their tomahawks and shields and did a war dance.
TRIBES:	*(They take tomahawks and shields and each form their own circle. They go to the right with a one-two-three beat, doing Indian dancing with raised tomahawks and giving war whoops. Then the tribes form straight lines at opposite ends of the room facing each other. They come forward and fight each other. Have a controlled fight—each person works out a fight pattern with their enemy so it doesn't become a free-for-all.)*
NARR.:	After much fierce fighting, the Bookeyes and the Library Hawks knew that if they kept up the fighting, soon there would be no more Library Indians. So they called a truce, and the chiefs got together to find a solution.
CHIEFS:	*(Talk together.)*

228

NARR.:	The chiefs talked for some time. Then it was decided that they would let the person-on-the-street decide whether fiction or non-fiction books were the best to read.
CHIEF B.:	*(Takes a pretend hand mike, and goes to the center, in front of the audience. The Bookeyes go to their small circle on one side of the room and the Hawkeyes go to their small circle on the other side.)*
CHIEF H.:	*(Stands with Chief Bookeye.)*
CHIEF B.:	Ladies and gentlemen, my name is Chief Bookeye, and I will be your Library Indian roving reporter. The subject today is Fiction and Non-fiction Books. Chief Hawkeye will help me with the interviews. The question is: Which do you think are more important—fiction, or non-fiction books?
CHIEF H.:	Look, Chief Bookeye, here comes our first person to interview.
PARENT:	*(In a hurry.)*
CHIEF B.:	If you please, [sir] [ma'am]. Stop a minute.
PARENT:	I'm in a hurry.
CHIEF B.:	I know, but Chief Hawkeye and I would like to ask you a quick question.
PARENT:	Well, as long as it's a quick question. I just cleaned the house. Now I have to shop for some supper, put the groceries away, make the supper, clean up after supper, and put the eight kids to bed—.
CHIEF H.:	Yes, yes. I understand. It will only take a minute of your time.
CHIEF B.:	The question is—which do you think more important—fiction or non-fiction books?
PARENT:	Well, let me see. Fiction is good.
BOOKEYES:	*(Shout, "Fiction!" and raise their hands)*
PARENT:	But, on the other hand, non-fiction is good, too.
HAWKS:	*(Shout, "Non-Fiction!" and raise their hands)*
CHIEF B.:	Which is the most important?
PARENT:	Which is what? I'm sorry, I don't know whether to have hot dogs or liver for supper.
HAWKS:	Hot dogs!
BOOKEYES:	Liver?! Boo!

CHIEF H.:	Which is more important—fiction or non-fiction books? Please, answer the question.
PARENT:	What do you mean by fiction?
CHIEF B.:	*(Getting disgusted.)* Fiction books are books that are not true.
PARENT:	You mean like fairy tales and novels and fantasies?
CHIEF H.:	Yes.
PARENT:	And non-fiction books are books of information? I like fiction books best. *(Hurries off.)*
CHIEF H.	Yes, [sir] [ma'am].
BOOKEYES:	*(They shout "Fiction!" and lift their hands.)*
CHIEF B.:	That's one for our side.
CHIEF H.:	Keep your feathers on, Chief Bookeye, here comes someone else we can question.
PROF.	*(Enters with books under arm.)*
CHIEF BOOKEYE:	Pardon me [sir] [ma'am], but you look like a learned person.
PROF.:	That I am. I am a Professor of Knowledge.
CHIEF H.:	Would you be good enough to answer a very important question for us?
PROF.:	Certainly. I'd be delighted.
CHIEF H.:	Which do you think are more important, fiction or non-fiction books?
PROF.:	Would you mind repeating the question?
CHIEF H.:	Which do you think are more important, fiction or non-fiction books?
PROF.:	Well, it depends.
CHIEF B.:	Depends on what?
PROF.:	Depends on all sorts of things. Now, you take—.
CHIEF B.:	Professor! Answer the question!
PROF.:	I never make hasty judgments.
CHIEF B.:	We can see that. We haven't got all day.
CHIEF H.:	*(Wearily.)* Do you have an answer to our question, Professor, or don't you?
PROF.:	Now that you mention it, I do.
CHIEF H.:	*(Shouts.)* What is it?
PROF.:	Being Professor of Knowledge...
CHIEFS:	Yes? Yes?
PROF.:	Non-fiction books are the most important. *(Exits.)*
HAWKS:	*(They shout, "Non-Fiction!" and wave their arms.)*

230

CHIEF H.:	So, that's one for our side.
CHIEF B.:	Here comes one more person.
LIB.:	*(Enters.)*
CHIEF B.:	Pardon me, [sir] [ma'am], we have a question to put to you.
LIB.:	What is your question?
CHIEF H.:	Which do you think are more important, fiction or non-fiction books?
LIB.:	Being a librarian, I think non-fiction books are important.
HAWKS & CHIEF H.:	*(They shout, "Non-Fiction!" and wave their hands.)* We won!
LIB.:	But, at the same time, I think fiction books are just as important as non-fiction books.
BOOKEYES & CHIEF B.:	*(Shout, "Fiction!" and wave their hands.)*
CHIEF B.:	We won, too.
CHIEF H.:	I guess you did.
LIB.:	A library is not complete without both fiction and non-fiction books. Readers are not fulfilled if they read only fiction or only non-fiction books. Facts and fantasy go hand-in-hand. *(Exits.)*
CHIEF B.:	[He's] [She's] right. Give me your hand, Chief Hawkeye.
CHIEF H.:	I give you my hand, Chief Bookeye. *(They shake hands.)*
CHIEF B.:	Let us pass the Book of Peace together.
TRIBES:	*(They form one big circle and the Book of Peace is passed, as a drum beat of 1-2-3-4 is sounded.)*
NARR.:	And so ends the story of the Bookeyes and the Library Hawks in the _____ Library. We hope you have enjoyed it. And everyone happily hereafter will read both fiction and non-fiction books.

The End

Grades 1–4, Long Program: Second Day

Materials Checklist

____ Indian name tags (from previous day)
____ sheets of Indian designs (from this book)—each child needs two
____ book about American Indians
____ film about American Indians
____ tomahawk pattern—have several
____ crayons and markers
____ paper
____ pencils
____ scissors
____ white glue
____ cardboard for tomahawks
____ stapler
____ animal crackers
____ milk
____ paper napkins
____ paper cups
____ scripts for play "Bookeyes and Library Hawks"
____ props for play (see page 227)

The Program

Goal

To learn more about the Indians.

Preparation

Photocopy the Indian designs on page 233, enough that each child will have two. Draw a tomahawk pattern about 20" long, make several copies and cut out.

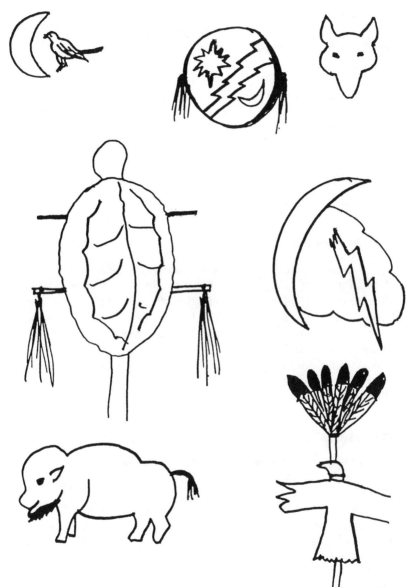

Indian designs

Library Indians

Getting Started   (Two groups, 15 minutes)

The Bookeyes and the Library Hawks are in their circles. Give out name tags and one sheet of Indian designs per person. Children color the Indian designs with their tribal colors. (They will use these designs later, in the craft activity.)

Story Time   (One group, 15 minutes)

The librarian reads a story about American Indians. (See Indian Book List.)

Library Time   (One group, 15 minutes)

Show a film about American Indians.

Indian Games   (One group, 15 minutes)

"Ten Little Indians." The children form a large circle. They start tow-heel ("Indian dancing") slowly around to the right. They chant: "One little, two little, three little Indians. Four little, five little, six little Indians. Seven little, eight little, nine little Indians. Ten little Library Indians." They repeat the chant two more times, each time picking up speed, so the last time they are chanting and dancing very fast.

Now the Indians dance backwards, and each time they are slower with the chanting and dancing. Finally they are back where they started. Use a drum or handclaps to keep the beat.

Indian Crafts   (Two groups, 30 minutes)

Tomahawks. The children trace the tomahawk pattern on a piece of heavy, white cardboard, and cut that out. (Make another cut-out for backing if the tomahawk is not strong enough.)

The children cut out the Indian designs they colored during "Getting Started." They glue these to the tomahawks. Add any other designs to the tomahawks, keeping the tribal colors, red and blue, the strongest. The children write their names on the tomahawks. Collect tomahawks. (To be used later in the play.)

Washup   (One group at a time, 5 minutes)

Snack (One group, 10 minutes)

Animal crackers and milk.

Indian Drama (One group, 30 minutes)

Rehearse the play, "Bookeyes and Library Hawks." Talk about the costumes and what each character should wear, and what to bring from home next time. Check props. Dress rehearsal is next time. Have lines learned, unless the librarian is to read the play.

Finishing Up (Two groups, 15 minutes)

Hand out second sheet of Indian designs. The children color these to take home.

Remind children and parents about Parents' Day.

Collect name tags.

Grades 1–4, Long Program: Third Day

Materials Checklist

____ Indian name tags (from previous days)
____ Indian masks (from this book)
____ crayons, markers, poster or acrylic paint
____ yarn
____ scissors
____ white glue
____ books on Indian art
____ modeling clay
____ chairs for game
____ heavy cardboard or large paper boxes
____ wide elastic or bands of cardboard
____ cut-up veggies
____ corn chips
____ V-8
____ paper cups
____ paper napkins
____ Indian makeup: blue, red, white, black, yellow
____ character makeup: blush, lipstick, black eyebrow pencil
____ Indian props: headbands, tomahawks and shields (headbands and
        tomahawks from previous day; shields will be made today)
____ other props for play (see page 227)
____ full headdresses or extra feathers for Chief Bookeye and Chief Hawk
____ bead necklaces for Chief Bookeye and Chief Hawk
____ scripts for play
____ tissues
____ cleansing cream
____ mirror
____ bobby pins

The Program

Goal

To learn about and appreciate Indian artwork and crafts.

Preparation

Photocopy and enlarge the blank Indian mask, page 238, one copy for each child. Make several copies of the completed Indian mask, page 238, and the Indian symbols, page 233.

Getting Started (Two groups, 15 minutes)

Give out name tags and Indian masks. Color Indian masks (with poster paint, crayons or markers) to take home. Show copies of completed Indian masks to give the children ideas for their coloring.

Story Time (One group, 15 minutes)

The librarian reads and shows the artwork from American Indian art books. (See Book List.)

Talk about American Indian art and crafts—clay pottery, bark baskets and canoes, totem poles, shell jewelry, cave drawings, feather work, etc.

Library Time (One group, 15 minutes)

Make a clay pot like one of the pictures in the American Indian art books. It doesn't have to be exact. Paint the pottery with Indian designs, using poster or acrylic paints. (Show Indian symbols.)

Indian Games (One group, 15 minutes)

"Who's Chief?" Chairs are set up in a line, every other one facing the opposite direction, as in musical chairs. There is one less chair than children. The Library Indians make a line around the chairs. A drum beat starts the war dance. The Library Indians dance around the chairs until the drum stops. They all try to sit in a chair. The one who has no chair is out. Another chair is taken away and the dance is repeated. The last Indian left with a chair sits in it and is proclaimed Chief.

Indian Crafts (Two groups, 30 minutes)

Indian Shields. Cut large circles from heavy cardboard or cardboard boxes, about 20 inches, one for each child. The children copy their name

Page 238: Blank Indian mask to color, and completed Indian mask.

237

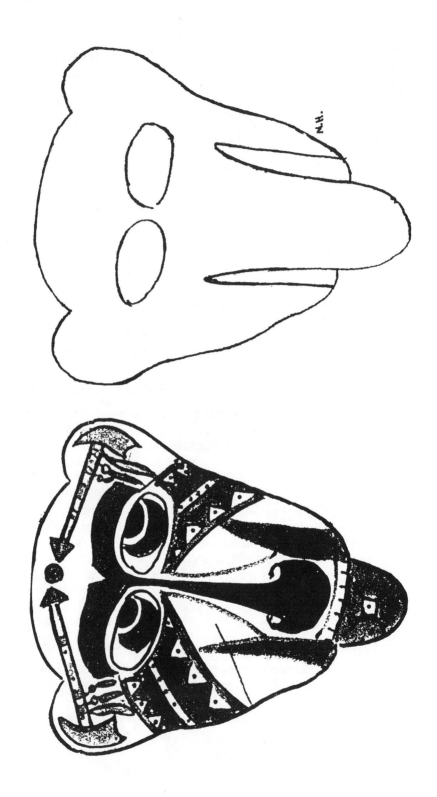

tag designs onto the circles, then paint them. Yarn fringe is added to Bookeyes. A piece of wide elastic is stapled across the middle of the back of the shield for the hand to go through to hold the shield. A cardboard strip or band stapled to the back is also good for a handle. The children write their names on the backs of the shields, and the shields are collected for the play. Now the children have headbands, tomahawks and shields for the play.

Washup   (One group at a time, 5 minutes)

Snack   (One group, 10 minutes)

Cut-up veggies (such as carrots & celery sticks), corn chips and V-8 juice.

Indian Drama   (One group, 30 minutes)

Dress rehearsal for the play, "Bookeyes and Library Hawks." Check all costumes and props.

Finishing Up   (Two groups, 15 minutes)

Try out the Indian makeup. Each tribe has its own predominant color— red or blue. Other colors are added, such as white, yellow, black. Makeup can be found at theatrical supply places, many drug stores and family bargain centers. Lipstick makes a great red; blue eyeshadow can be used for the blue, and black eyebrow pencil for the black, if no theatrical makeup is available. See completed masks, page 238, for ideas in doing makeup. For an easy design, run a line of red or blue from the middle of the forehead down to the end of the nose. Make two lines along the cheekbone with the red or blue. Fill in between the two red or blue lines with X's of other colors or dots. Run two black lines across the forehead, and add red or blue X's or dots. Have plenty of tissues, cleansing cream, and mirrors, for taking off makeup, and bobby pins for pinning on the headbands. Also do the makeup for the characters.

Chiefs should have more feathers in the headband, or full headdresses. Ask the children and parents for these. Someone always has an Indian head-dress and beads. (Try Scouts.) Ask the children to bring any Indian items they might have at home. Leather vests and necklaces are great. Make the people who are interviewed funny characters—glasses, hats, crazy clothes, etc.

Remind parents about the play. Ask a friend to attend.

Collect name tags.

Grades 1–4, Long Program: Fourth Day

Materials Checklist

____ Indian name tags (from previous days)
____ materials for writing a play—paper, pencils, books on playwriting
____ a play to read for Story Time
____ Library Indian paper dolls (from this book)—enough for group
____ scissors
____ white glue
____ cardboard for paper doll backing (optional)
____ markers and crayons
____ scripts, props, costumes, makeup for play "Bookeyes and Library Hawks"
____ chairs for Parents' Day audience
____ corn muffins or cupcakes
____ butter (if serving corn muffins)
____ fruit drink
____ paper cups
____ paper napkins

The Program

Goal

To experience writing and performing plays.

Preparation

Photocopy the Indian paper dolls and clothes, pages 241–242, a set for each child. Set up chairs for Parents' Day audience. You may wish to bake your own corn muffins or cupcakes ahead of time (but bakery-purchased will do).

Clothes for Library Indian paper doll.

241

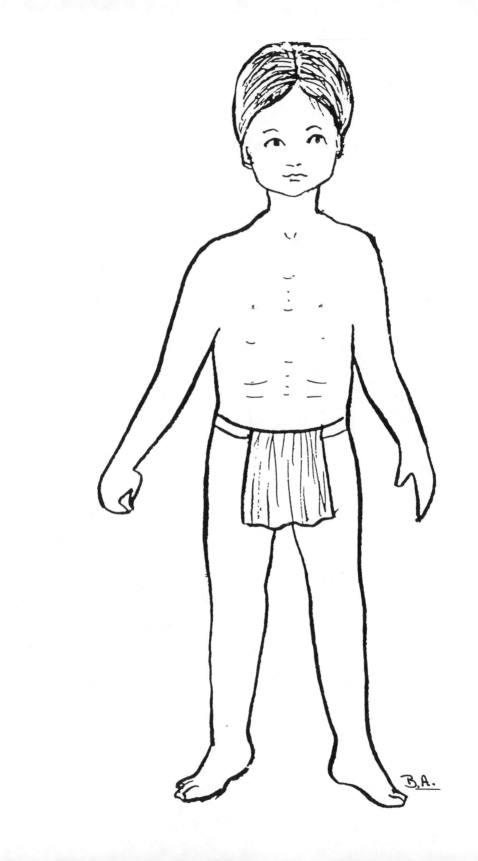

Getting Started (Two groups, 15 minutes)

Give out name tags.

Talk about writing a play. Has anyone ever written a play? If so, talk about it. How is a play different from a story? (The characters have to do the talking and acting in person.) There is dialogue (talking). Everything happens in front of an audience—live, not like TV. Everything has to be clear. In a play the audience has to be with the actors, be a part of the play. You can't have a retake if you goof in a play. An actor must speak loudly and clearly.

A playwright, the one who writes the play, is very important. Without a playwright, there would be no play. The actors depend on a playwright to write them good lines and actions, to help them be good actors and make the audience enjoy the play. Can you name any playwrights?

Story Time (One group, 15 minutes)

The librarian reads a play to the children.

Library Time (One group, 15 minutes)

Read about playwriting from playwriting books. Talk more about writing a play. Give out paper and pencils. Ask the children to write a short play. The fewer the characters, the simpler the play. Have a problem to solve in the play. Each child could write his own, or the group could write one together.

Indian Crafts (Two groups, 30 minutes)

Indian Paper Dolls. Hand out the Library Indian paper dolls and clothes that have been photocopied from this book. The doll can be used as a boy Indian. Perhaps the children would enjoy making him some clothes. Adding the hair and clothes provided, the doll becomes a girl doll. The children color them and cut them out. Remember, do not cut off the tabs on the clothes. Use a cardboard backing to make the paper dolls stronger (optional). These paper dolls can be made into stickpuppets by gluing tongue depressors, Popsicle sticks, or straws to the back.

Washup (One group at a time, 5 minutes)

Snack (One group, 10 minutes)

Corn muffins and butter, or cupcakes, and fruit drink.

243

Indian Drama (One group, 30 minutes)

Present the play "Bookeyes and Library Hawks."

Finishing Up (Two groups, 15 minutes)

Take off makeup and costumes. Talk about the play.

Tell the children they were wonderful actors and playwrights. Read (some of) the play(s) the children wrote at Library Time.

Tell the children to come often to the library, as the library is their special place.

Children take home name tags, crafts, etc.

Library Indians:
Grades 1–4, Short Program
Time: 2 days; 1 1/2 hours each day

Getting Started: Indian name tags (10 min.)
Story Time: Book about American Indians (10 min.)
Library Time: Library Tour (10 min.)
Indian Games: "Sand Painting to Music" (10 min.)
Indian Crafts: Indian Headbands (10 min.)
Washup and Snack: Corn chips, fruit juice (15 min.)
Indian Drama: "Bookeyes and Library Hawks"—read-through and practice (15 min.)
Finishing Up: Indian Necklace (10 min.)

Getting Started: Make tomahawks (10 min.)
Story Time: Book about American Indians (10 min.)
Library Time: Film about Indians (10 min.)
Indian Games: "The Indian Card Catalog Game" (10 min.)
Indian Crafts: Library Indian Paper Dolls (10 min.)
Washup and Snack: Popcorn and apple juice (15 min.)
Indian Drama: Present "Bookeyes and Library Hawks" (15 min.)
Finishing Up (10 min.)

Grades 1–4, Short Program: First Day

Materials Checklist

____ Indian name tags (from this book)
____ white cardboard
____ yarn—blue and red
____ small brushes
____ varnish
____ books on American Indians
____ tape or record of Indian-sounding music
____ tape or record player
____ long, white sheet of shelf paper
____ salt shakers filled with sand (one for each child)
____ crayons, markers and poster paints
____ white glue
____ scissors
____ paper punch
____ stapler
____ construction paper for headbands (white and colors)
____ feathers (optional)
____ corn chips
____ fruit juice
____ paper cups
____ paper napkins
____ scripts for librarian and assistant for the play "Bookeyes and Library Hawks"
____ props and costumes for play (see page 227)

The Program

Goals

To learn about the American Indians, and to get to know the library.

Preparation

Enlarge (by hand or on copier) the Indian name tags on page 280. (You may prefer to use them actual size.) Each child will need a copy of the appropriate tag for his or her age group ("Bookeyes," Grades 1–2; "Library Hawks," Grades 3–4). You may wish to further prepare name tags for Grades 1–2 by cutting them out, punching holes and threading yarn. Make two copies of the play, "Bookeyes and Library Hawks," pages 227–231.

Getting Started   (Two groups,* 10 minutes)

The Bookeyes, Grades 1–2, and the Library Hawks, Grades 3–4, are in their Indian circles. Give out Indian name tags to color. Punch a hole at the top of the Indian shield for red (Bookeyes) or blue (Library Hawks) yarn to go through. Make yarn long to go over a child's head. Children write their names on the name tags.

Story Time   (One group, 10 minutes)

The children sit around the librarian, who reads them a book about American Indians. (See Indian Book List.)

Library Time   (Two groups, 10 minutes)

Take a short tour of the library. Point out interesting things—card catalog, new arrivals, Indian books, displays, etc. While one group is touring, a story about Indians is read to the other group. When all are back together again, talk about the things they saw in the library. Who can remember the most things?

Indian Games   (One group, 10 minutes)

"Sand Painting to Music." Roll out a long sheet of white shelf paper on the floor. The children kneel on all sides of the paper. Each child has a marker or crayon. (Poster paints make a stronger painting, but they do get messy.) Tell the children that when the Indian music begins (a drum is fine, too) they are to make an Indian design on the paper. (Show some of the Indian designs and symbols from this book, page 233.) When the music stops, they are to

*"Two groups" notation signifies that division of a large group is appropriate or desirable for an activity. You may prefer not to divide small groups.

change colors and places with someone else. Start the music again and make another design. Do this until there are enough designs to make a picture. Then the children spread white glue on their designs and sprinkle sand on the glue. Let dry and then hang up on the wall.

Indian Crafts   (Two groups, 10 minutes)

Indian Headbands. See "Indian Crafts," page 226.

Washup   (One group at a time, 5 minutes)

Snack   (One group, 10 minutes)

Corn chips tied up in a paper napkin, fruit juice.

Indian Drama   (One group, 15 minutes)

Read through the play "Bookeyes and Library Hawks" and choose the characters. The librarian reads the lines unless the children wish to learn the lines in a short time, or they listen to the play enough to ad lib. Talk about ad libbing (making up as you go). Rehearse the play as long as there is time. Check costumes, props and makeup.

Finishing Up   (Two groups, 10 minutes)

Make an Indian necklace: Children cut four rectangles of white cardboard about 2" long and 1" wide. Then cut out one rectangle larger than the others. These rectangles will be beads for the necklace. Decorate the rectangle beads with Indian designs. (Show page 233.) Tie the larger rectangle bead in the center on a piece of yarn about 21 inches long. Then tie two of the rectangle beads about 1" away on either side of the center bead, and tie each of the other two rectangle beads 1" further away. Varnish the front of the beads and let dry. Keep necklaces for the play. Children write their names on the back of the center bead.

Tell the children to bring a friend or parent to see the play.

Collect name tags.

248

Grades 1–4, Short Program: Second Day

Materials Checklist

____ Indian name tags (from previous day)
____ books on American Indians
____ tomahawk pattern — have several
____ sheets of Indian designs (from this book)
____ film about American Indians
____ Library Indian paper dolls (from this book) — each child needs a set
____ cardboard backing for paper dolls (optional)
____ popcorn
____ apple juice
____ paper napkins
____ paper cups
____ scissors
____ white glue
____ crayons and markers
____ stapler
____ scripts, costumes, makeup, and props for play (see page 227)
____ chairs for Parents' Day audience
____ tissues
____ cleansing cream
____ mirror
____ bobby pins

The Program

Goals

To learn more about libraries and Indians, and to give the children the experience of working together in a play.

Preparation

Prepare a tomahawk pattern (see page 232). Photocopy the Indian designs on page 233 — one copy per child. Photocopy the Library Indian paper dolls and clothes, pages 241 and 242 — each child needs one copy of each page. Set up chairs for Parents' Day audience.

Getting Started   (Two groups, 10 minutes)

Give out Indian name tags and sheets of designs. Children color Indian designs. Then the children make tomahawks to be used in the play: see "Indian Crafts," page 234.

Story Time   (One group, 10 minutes)

The librarian reads a story about American Indians.

Library Time   (One group, 10 minutes)

Show a film about American Indians.

Indian Games   (One group, 10 minutes)

Talk about the card catalog. Play "The Indian Card Catalog Game." The Library Indians take turns looking up a book about animals in the card catalog and reading the title to the group. Each chooses an animal to look up that an Indian would know. (Ask: Why would an elephant not be chosen?) An animal may be picked more than once, but each child must find a different book title. The children are timed, and the one who finds and reads a title fastest is the winner. If there is a large number and all cannot have a turn, have the children pick six or ten warriors from their tribe to go on the book title hunt for them.

Indian Crafts   (Two groups, 15 minutes)

Library Indian Paper Dolls. Each child has a set of the Library Indian paper dolls to color and cut out. Cardboard backing may be added to the dolls for more support (optional). Be sure not to cut off the tabs on the clothes.

Washup   (One group at a time, 5 minutes)

Snack

Place a handful of popcorn in a paper napkin and tie shut. Serve apple juice.

Indian Drama   (One group, 15 minutes)

Present the play "Bookeyes and Library Hawks." (If more time is needed for the play, omit Story Time.) The children love being made up, so use five minutes to do this. The parents will help with makeup and costumes. Keep costumes of characters simple. The children wear their headbands, necklaces and carry their tomahawks. A drum adds greatly to the play.

Finishing Up   (Two groups, 5 minutes)

Take off makeup. Have tissues and cleansing cream on hand. Talk about the play.

Tell the children they were great Library Indians, and ask them to come often to the library.

Children take home crafts, name tags, etc.

Library Indians:
Preschool–Kindergarten, Long Program
Time: 2 days; 1 1/2 hours each day

Getting Started: Indian name tags (10 min.)
Story Time: Book about American Indians (10 min.)
Library Time: Library tour / Library Indian girl paper doll (10 min.)
Indian Games: "Give the Indian Girl a Book" (5 min.)
Indian Crafts: Indian Headbands (15 min.)
Washup and Snack: Apple halves, raisins (drink optional) (15 min.)
Indian Drama: "The Iroquois"—read-through and practice (15 min.)
Finishing Up: (10 min.)

SECOND DAY
Getting Started: Library Indian boy paper doll (10 min.)
Library Time: Film about American Indians (10 min.)
Indian Games: "Indian Dancing" (5 min.)
Washup and Snack: Corn bread and butter, V-8 (10 min.)
Indian Drama: Present "The Iroquois" (15 min.)
Finishing Up (10 min.)

Preschool–Kindergarten, Long Program:
First Day

Materials Checklist

____ Indian name tags (from this book)
____ red and blue yarn for name tags
____ cardboard backing for name tags (optional)
____ scissors
____ white glue
____ crayons and markers
____ paper punch
____ book about American Indians
____ Indian Games Girl (from this book)
____ paper book for game (see "Indian Games")
____ blindfold
____ tape, pins or stapler
____ apples
____ raisins
____ drink (optional)
____ paper napkins
____ paper cups (optional)
____ two copies of play, "The Iroquois" (from this book)

The Program

Goal

To learn about the American Indian, especially the Iroquois.

Preparation

Photocopy the Indian name tags, page 224—each child will need one. For this age group you may want to prepare the name tags further (see "Getting Started") so that children only color and write names. Photocopy the Library Indian girl paper doll and clothes, pages 241–242, enough for group (each child needs full set). Enlarge (by hand or on copier) the Indian Girl, page 256; color, cut out, and attach to wall for Indian Games. Make the copies of the play, "The Iroquois," pages 257–259—one for librarian, one for assistant.

Cut apples in half (each child will get one half).

Getting Started   (Two groups,* 10 minutes)

The children are in two Indian circles. Preschoolers are the Red Chiefs and kindergarteners are the Blue Chiefs. Name tags are given to each child to color. Cut them out. Attach to cardboard backing (optional), punch hole in top, and thread red or blue yarn through hole. Yarn should go around child's neck. Tie ends of yarn together.

Story Time   (One group, 10 minutes)

The two tribes are together for Story Time. The librarian reads a book about American Indians.

Talk about Indians. Do you have any Indian friends? Do you feel sorry for the American Indians? Why? Who was here first—the Indians or the white settlers? The Indians respected nature. What are people doing now to hurt nature?

The Indians made beautiful pottery, baskets, jewelry. They made birch bark canoes. Were the Indians friendly when Columbus landed here? (Etc.)

Library Time   (Two groups, 10 minutes)

Take a tour of the library. Show the children where books about Indians are located. While one group is touring, the children of the other group color the Indian Girl paper doll. They cut out the paper doll and clothes. Remember, do not cut off the tabs on the clothes.

---

*"Two groups" notation signifies that division is appropriate or desirable for a large group. You may prefer not to divide small groups.

Indian Games   (One group, 5 minutes)

"Give the Indian Girl a book." The children line up in front of the Indian Girl drawing, which has been attached to the wall. The first child is blindfolded (as in Pin the Tail on the Donkey.) The idea is for the children to try to pin or tape a paper book as near as they can to the book in the Indian Girl's hands. The one closest is the winner.

Indian Crafts   (Two groups, 15 minutes)

Indian Headbands. See "Indian Crafts," page 226.

Washup   (One group at a time, 5 minutes)

Snack   (One group, 10 minutes)

Each child has a half an apple and some raisins in a paper napkin. Drink is optional.

Indian Drama   (One group, 15 minutes)

Read through the play, "The Iroquois." Have the children act out the play. Choose the characters or actors. Go over the play as long as there is time.

Finishing Up   (Two groups, 10 minutes)

Encourage the children to bring any Indian objects they may have at home for next time. Tell them to invite their parents to see the play at the next session.

Collect name tags and headbands.

The Iroquois

A Preschool and Kindergarten Play
by
Taffy Jones

Characters:

LIBRARIAN
MOHAWK
ONEIDA
ONONDAGA
CAYUGA
SENECA
TUSCARORA
WHITE SETTLERS

Props:

Indian makeup (optional)
Indian headbands, tomahawks (these are made during craft periods)
six bead necklaces

The play takes place at the Mohawk campfire.

LIBRARIAN:	The tribes that formed the Iroquois Confederacy were the most powerful in the Northeast. They lived where New York State is today, and they were feared even beyond their territory. The Iroquois were made up of the Mohawks...
MOHAWK:	*(Enters and stands facing the audience.)* I am Mohawk.
LIBRARIAN:	The Oneidas...
ONEIDA:	*(Enters and stands next to Mohawk.)* I am Oneida.
LIBRARIAN:	The Onondagas...
ONONDAGA:	*(Enters and stands next to Oneida.)* I am Onondaga.

Opposite: Indian girl (for "Indian Games")—enlarge.

257

LIBRARIAN:	The Cayugas...
CAYUGA:	*(Enters and stands next to Onondaga.)* I am Cayuga.
LIBRARIAN:	The Senecas...
SENECA:	*(Enters and stands next to Cayuga.)* I am Seneca.
LIBRARIAN:	These five tribes made up the Iroquois. These tribes were known as the Woodland Indians. The forest to them was a woodland friend. They lived in bark houses called "long houses," in which several families of the tribe lived together, though each family had its own cooking fire. They were known as "People of the Long Houses." Who were known as People of the Long Houses? Who were these five tribes of the Iroquois?
TRIBES:	*(Each tribe says name, one after the other, very slowly.)*
LIBRARIAN:	These five tribes of the Iroquois did not get along. They fought each other. Who didn't get along?
TRIBES:	*(Each tribe says name one after the other, but faster this time. They do a mock fight—a little pushing—with the tribe next to them.)*
LIBRARIAN:	Soon, they were weakening each other with all the fighting. Other Indian tribes now came and attacked them. Who was fighting and fighting?
TRIBES:	*(Each tribe says name one after the other, but much faster. They fight each other with raised tomahawks.)*
LIBRARIAN:	A Peace Plan was drawn up and the Iroquois no longer fought each other. They were brothers and sisters helping brothers and sisters. Who were brothers and sisters helping brothers and sisters?
TRIBES:	*(Each tribe says name one after the other, but at normal speed. The first two face each other, as do the next two. Each puts his or her right hand on the right shoulder of the opposite person. This leaves one Indian standing alone.)*
LIBRARIAN:	Then, the Iroquois added the Tuscaroras to their confederacy. Now there were six nations.
TUSCARORA:	*(Enters and faces the Indian standing alone. They put their right hands on each other's shoulders.)*

258

LIBRARIAN: Now who made up the Iroquois?

TRIBES: *(Each says name, one after another.)*

LIBRARIAN: Each tribe gives another wampum.

TRIBES: *(Each places a bead necklace over the head of the Indian to the right. The last Indian walks around to place necklace over head of first Indian.)*

LIBRARIAN: Wampum or shell necklaces were very special to the Iroquois Indians. So this was a special time for whom?

TRIBES: *(Say names, one after the other.)*

LIBRARIAN: The white settlers came and there was much fighting, and soon the Indians disappeared one by one. Today, only a few of the proud and powerful Iroquois remain.

SETTLERS: *(Enter. They push all the Indians off stage. Then they stand facing the audience.)*

LIBRARIAN: The Indians were the first people of our land. They lost their land to the settlers. The heartbreak of the once-proud Indians will never be forgotten.

SETTLERS: *(Exit.)*

The End

Preschool–Kindergarten, Long Program:
Second Day

Materials Checklist

____ Indian name tags (from previous day)
____ book about American Indians
____ film about American Indians
____ drums for Indian Dancing
____ tomahawk pattern—have several
____ sheets of Indian designs (from this book)—one per child
____ corn bread
____ V-8
____ paper napkins
____ paper cups
____ scripts, costumes and makeup for the play, "The Iroquois"
____ chairs for Parents' Day audience
____ scissors
____ white glue
____ stapler
____ tape
____ crayons and markers
____ cardboard
____ Library Indian paper doll (from this book)
____ tissues
____ cleansing cream
____ mirror
____ bobby pins (to hold headbands in place)

The Program

Goal

To learn more about Indians, and to present play for audience.

Preparation

See instructions for the tomahawk pattern on page 232; make several copies and cut out. Photocopy the Indian designs on page 233—one copy for each child. Photocopy the Library Indian boy/girl paper doll and clothes, pages 241–242—enough for group. You may wish to bake your own cornbread ahead of time. Set up chairs for Parents' Day audience.

Getting Started (Two groups, 10 minutes)

Name tags and Library Indian boy/girl paper dolls are given out. The children color and cut out the paper doll and clothes. Remember, do not cut off the tabs on the clothes.

Story Time (One group, 10 minutes)

Book About American Indians. (See Indian Book List.)

Library Time (One group, 10 minutes)

Show a film about American Indians.

Indian Games (One group, 5 minutes)

Do Indian dancing with drums. Indians go toe-heel, toe-heel around in a circle, using their bodies to move down to the ground and up. On toe, bend down, and on heel, come up. Repeat this dance to the drum beat 1-2, 1-2. Then the beat gets stronger than the first beat—1-2-3, 1-2-3. The children bring their toes and heels down on the one, then on the two, three, they stomp twice with their right foot. Repeat with the left foot, and then go back to the right foot and repeat.

Indian Crafts (Two groups, 15 minutes)

Tomahawks. Pass out Indian designs and tomahawk patterns. Children color Indian designs. To make tomahawk, see "Indian Crafts," page 234.

Washup (One group at a time, 5 minutes)

Snack   (One group, 10 minutes)

Corn bread and butter, V-8 juice.

Indian Drama   (One group, 15 minutes)

Put on Indian makeup (see "Finishing Up," page 239, for suggestions.) Parents can help. Present the play, "The Iroquois," for parents.

Finishing Up   (Two groups, 10 minutes)

Talk about the play. Take off makeup.

Tell the children there are many interesting subjects like the American Indians found in books in the library. Invite them to come often and take out exciting books to read.

Children take costumes, crafts and name tags home.

Library Indians:
Preschool–Kindergarten, Short Program
Time: 1 day; 1 1/2 hours

Getting Started: Indian name tags (10 min.)
Story Time: Book about American Indians (10 min.)
Library Time: Library tour / Indian Dancing (10 min.)
Indian Games: "Indian Drumming" (5 min.)
Indian Crafts: Indian Headbands (15 min.)
Washup and Snack: Corn chips, V-8 (15 min.)
Indian Drama: "The Iroquois" (15 min.)
Finishing Up: (10 min.)

Materials Checklist

____ Indian name tags (from this book)
____ red and blue yarn for name tags
____ scissors
____ crayons and markers
____ book about American Indians
____ two copies of play, "The Iroquois" (from this book)
____ construction paper
____ white glue
____ corn chips
____ fruit juice
____ paper napkins
____ paper cups
____ Indian makeup—red lipstick, black eyebrow pencil, blue eyeshadow
      (or use theatrical makeup)
____ drum
____ bead necklaces for play (six)

The Program

Goals

To think about the library as a special place; to work with others and gain self-confidence.

Preparation

Photocopy the Indian name tags, page 224, one for each child. You may wish to prepare name tags further for this age group. (See page 254.) Make two copies of the play, "The Iroquois," pages 257–259 (one for librarian, one for an assistant).

Getting Started   (Two groups,* 10 minutes)

See "Getting Started," page 254.

Story Time   (One group, 10 minutes)

The two Indian tribes join together for Story Time. The librarian reads them a story about American Indians (especially the Iroquois).

Library Time   (Two groups, 10 minutes)

One tribe tours the library while the other tribe does Indian Dancing. (See "Indian Games," page 261.)

Indian Games   (One group, 5 minutes)

"Indian Drumming." The children sit in a large circle. A drum is passed from one child to another. Each child takes a turn beating the drum. He or she starts with steady beats, 1-2-3-4-5-6-7-8, then passes the drum to the person on his or her right. That child likewise beats the drum for eight beats. When back to the beginning, do series of four beats with emphasis on the first: 1-2-3-4, 1-2-3-4. This is repeated all around the circle. Then the first

*"Two groups" notation signifies that division is appropriate or desirable for a large group. You may not wish to divide small groups.

264

child gets up and Indian dances as he or she drums. The drum is passed to the next Indian until all have Indian Danced.

Indian Crafts   (Two groups, 15 minutes)

Indian Headbands. See "Indian Crafts," page 261.

Washup   (One group at a time, 5 minutes)

Snack   (One group, 10 minutes)

Corn chips and V-8 juice. Put a handful of corn chips in a paper napkin and tie. Serve juice in paper cups.

Indian Drama   (One group, 15 minutes)

Put on Indian makeup. Use mostly red lipstick on the Red Chiefs and mostly blue eyeshadow on the Blue Chiefs. Put a small amount of the other color on the other tribe. Outline and highlight with black eyebrow pencil. Put on Indian headbands. Read and act out play, "The Iroquois." (Note: Since this group does not have time to make tomahawks, children can pantomime using tomahawks in fight scene.)

Finishing Up   (Two groups, 10 minutes)

Tell the children they have been wonderful Library Indians, and invite them to come often to the library. It is their special place to be. Tell them to watch TV, then read a book. Children take home crafts, name tags, etc.

Indian Totem Pole

If you wish to make a totem pole, enlarge and photocopy the Indian designs on the next two pages. Repeat the designs to make as tall a totem pole as desired. For each section of the pole, roll colored cardboard (22" by 28" sections work well) into a tube. Glue the designs, after they have been painted or colored to the front of the tube. Stack sections as high as desired and tape together.

L.H.

Totem pole pattern (enlarge to twice as big).

267

Totem pole pattern (enlarge to twice as big).

Bibliography

Bears Book List

Alexander, Martha. *Blackboard Bear.* New York: Dial, 1969.

Allen, Pamela. *Bertie and the Bear.* New York: Coward, McCann 1983.

Asch, Frank. *Sand Cake.* New York: Parents Magazine Press, 1978.

Bach, Alice. *Smartest Bear and His Brother Oliver.* New York: Harper and Row, 1975.

Berenstain, Stanley and Janice. The Berenstains are the authors of a well-loved series of books about a bear family, including *Bears' Picnic, Bears' Vacation,* and *The Berenstain Bears' New Baby.* All are published by Random House of New York, some under the Beginner imprint.

Bethell, Jean. *Look Who's Taking a Bath.* New York: Scholastic, 1979.

Bond, Michael. *A Bear Called Paddington.* New York: Dell, 1968. Paddington Bear is the star of an extensive series by Bond; this is the first volume.

Freeman, Don. *Corduroy.* New York: Viking, 1968.

Gackenbach, Dick. *Poppy the Panda.* New York: Clarion, 1984.

Ginsburg, Mira. *Two Greedy Bears.* Illustrated by Jose Aruego and Adriane Dewey. New York: Macmillan, 1976.

Jeschke, Susan. *Angela and Bear.* New York: Holt, 1979.

McCloskey, Robert. *Blueberries for Sal.* New York: Viking, 1948.

Martin, Bill, Jr. *Brown Bear, Brown Bear, What Do You See?* Illustrated by Eric Carle. New York: Holt, Rinehart and Winston, 1967.

Milne, A. A. *Winnie the Poo.* New York: Dutton, 1971 (reprint).

Mogensen, Jan. *When Teddy Woke Early.* Milwaukee: Gareth Stevens, 1985. Other Teddy books are available.

Pryor, Bonnie. *Grandpa Bear.* Illustrated by Bruce Degen. New York: Morrow, 1986.

Reinach, Jacquelyn. *Scaredy Bear.* New York: Holt, Rinehart and Winston, 1978.

Schlachter, Rita. *Bear Needs Help!* Illustrated by Patti Boyd. Mahwah NJ: Troll Associates, 1986.

Steiner, Jorg. *The Bear Who Wanted to Be a Bear.* Illustrated by Jorg Muller. New York: Atheneum, 1976.

Weinberg, Laurence. *The Forgetful Bears.* New York: Scholastic, 1981.

Mice and Cats Book List

Calhoun, Mary. *Audubon Cat.* New York: Morrow, 1981.
Carter, Angela. *Comic and Curious Cats.* new York: Crown, 1979.
Freeman, Don. *Norman the Doorman.* New York: Viking, 1959.
Gag, Wanda. *Millions of Cats.* New York: Coward, 1928.
Kraus, Robert. *Whose Mouse Are You?* Illustrated by Jose Aruego. New York: Greenwillow, 1972.
————. *Where Are You Going, Little Mouse?* Illustrated by Jose Aruego and Adriane Dewey. New York: Greenwillow, 1986.
Lionni, Leo. *Frederick.* New York: Pantheon, 1966. There are other mouse stories by this author.
Lobel, Arnold. *Mouse Tales.* New York: Harper and Row, 1972.
————. *Mouse Soup.* New York: Harper and Row, 1977.
Mayer, Mercer. *The Great Cat Chase.* New York: Scholastic, 1975.
Miller, Edna. *Mousekin Finds a Friend.* (Series.) Englewood Cliffs NJ: Prentice Hall, 1967.
Miller, Moira. *Oscar Mouse Finds a Home.* Illustrated by Marici Majewska. New York: Dial, 1985.
Newberry, Clare Turlay. *April's Kittens.* New York: Harper, 1940.
Numeroff, Laura Joffe. *If You Give a Mouse a Cookie.* Illustrated by Felicia Bond. New York: Harper and Row, 1985.
Dr. Seuss. *The Cat in the Hat.* New York: Beginner, 1957.
Titus, Eve. *Anatole and the Cat.* New York: McGraw-Hill, 1957.

Bookworm Book List

Aheberg, Janet and Allan. *The Little Worm Book.* New York: Viking, 1980.
Carle, Eric. *The Very Hungry Caterpillar.* New York: Philomel, 1970.
Craig, Paula M. *Mr. Wiggle's Book.* Minneapolis: Denison, 1972.
Darling, Lois and Louis. *Worms.* New York: Morrow, 1972.
Hess, Lilo. *The Amazing Earthworm.* New York: Scribner's, 1979.
Hogan, Paula Z. *The Life Cycle of the Butterfly.* Illustrated by Geri K. Strigenz. New York: Raintree, 1979.
Hogner, Dorothy Childs. *Earthworms.* Illustrated by Nils Hogner. New York: Crowell, 1953.
Lionni, Leo. *Inch by Inch.* Obolensky, 1962.
McClung, Robert M. *Caterpillars — and How They Live.* New York: Morrow, 1965.
Rockwell, Thomas. *How to Eat Fried Worms.* New York: Watts, 1972.
Wong, Herbert H., and Vessel, Matthew F. *Our Caterpillars.* Illustrated by Aris Stewart Wesley. Reading MA: Addison-Wesley.

Hat Book List

Blos, Joan W. *Martin's Hats.* Illustrated by Marc Simont. New York: Morrow, 1984.

Geringer, Laura. *Three Hat Day*. Pictures by Arnold Lobel. New York: Harper and Row, 1985.

Hall, William. *The Walking Hat*. Pictures by Kurt Wiese. New York: Knopf, 1950.

Keats, Ezra Jack. *Jennie's Hat*. New York: Harper and Row, 1966.

Murphey, Sara. *The Animal Hat Shop*. Chicago: Follett, 1964.

Dr. Seuss. *The Cat in the Hat*. New York: Random House, 1957.

Dinosaur Book List

Aliki. *My Visit to the Dinosaurs*. New York: Crowell, 1969.

————. *Dinosaurs Are Different*. New York: Harper and Row, 1985.

Andrews, Roy. *All About Dinosaurs*. New York: Random House, 1953.

Berg, Cherney. *Three-horn the Dinosaur*. Educational Reading Services, 1970.

Bram, Elizabeth. *A Dinosaur Is Too Big*. New York: Greenwillow, 1977.

Carrick, Carol. *What Happened to Patrick's Dinosaur?* Illustrated by Donald Carrick. New York: Clarion, 1986.

Cole, Joanna. *Dinosaur Story*. New York: Morrow, 1974.

Hoff, Syd. *Danny and the Dinosaur*. New York: Harper, 1958.

Kellogg, Steven. *The Mysterious Tadpole*. New York: Dial, 1977.

Kingdon, Jill. *The Dinosaur Counting Book*. Delair, 1984.

Klein, Norma. *Dinosaur's Housewarming Party*. New York: Crown, 1974.

Kroll, Steven. *The Tyrannosaurus Game*. New York: Holiday, 1976.

La Placa, Michael. *How to Draw Dinosaurs*. Albertson NY: Watermill, 1982.

Logan, Richard. *Thunder the Dinosaur Books*. (Series.) Glendale CA: Cypress, 1977.

Martin, Rodney. *There's a Dinosaur in the Park*. Illustrated by John Siow. Milwaukee: Gareth Stevens, 1987.

Matthews, Williams H., III. *Wonders of the Dinosaur World*. New York: Dodd, Mead, 1963.

Parish, Peggy. *Dinosaur Time*. New York: Harper and Row, 1974.

Parker, Steve. *The Age of Dinosaurs*. Milwaukee: Gareth Stevens, 1985.

Sterne, Noelle. *Tyrannosaurus Wrecks: A Book of Dinosaur Riddles*. New York: Crowell, 1979.

Young, Miriam. *If I Rode a Dinosaur*. New York: Lothrop, Lee and Shepard, 1974.

Indian Book List

Batherman, Muriel. *Indians of North America*. Boston: Houghton Mifflin, 1981.

Blood, Charles L. *American Indian Games and Crafts*. New York: Watts, 1981.

Cooke, David C., and Moyers, William. *Famous Indian Tribes*. New York: Random House, 1954.

Goble, Paul. *The Girl Who Loved Horses*. New York: Bradbury, 1960.

————. *Star Boy*. New York: Bradbury, 1983.

Gorsline, Marie. *North American Indians*. New York: Random House, 1977.

Hofsinde, Robert (Gray Wolf). *The Indian's Secret World*. New York: Morrow, 1955.

Indians of North America. American Heritage Junior Books Series. Racine WI: Golden, 1960.

La Farge, Oliver. *The American Indian*. Racine WI: Golden, 1960

McNeer, May. *The American Indian Story*. Illustrated by Lynd Ward. New York: Farrar, Straus and Giroux, 1963.
Songs and Stories of the North American Indians. New York: Grosset and Dunlap, 1968.
Speare, Elizabeth George. *The Sign of the Beaver*. Boston: Houghton Mifflin, 1983.
White, Anne Terry. *The American Indian*. New York: Random House, 1963.

Poetry Book List

Dickinson, Emily. *I'm Nobody! Who Are You?* Owings Mills MD: Stemmer House, 1978.
Fujikawa, Gyo. *Come Follow Me*. New York: Grosset and Dunlap, 1979.
Jones, Charla. *Poetry Patterns*. O'Fallon MO: Book Lures, 1985.
Koch, Kenneth. *Rose Where Did You Get So Red?* New York: Random House, 1973.
McCord, David. *All Small*. Illustrated by Madelaine Gill Linden. Boston: Little, Brown, 1986.
O'Neill, Mary. *Hailstones and Halibut Bones*. Garden City NY: Doubleday, 1961.
Prelutsky, Jack. *It's Snowing! It's Snowing!* New York: Greenwillow, 1984.
————. *My Parents Think I'm Sleeping*. New York: Greenwillow, 1985.
Silverstein, Shel. *Where the Sidewalk Ends*. New York: Harper and Row, 1974.
Viorst, Judith. *If I Were in Charge of the World*. Illustrated by Lynne Cherry. New York: Atheneum, 1981.

Puppet Book List

Adair, Margaret Weeks. *Do-It-in-a-Day Puppets: for Beginners*. New York: John Day, 1964.
Baird, Bill. *The Art of the Puppet*. New York: Macmillan, 1965.
Champlin, Connie. *Puppetry and Creative Dramatics in Storytelling*. Illustrated by Nancy Renfro. Nancy Renfro Studios, 1980.
Chesse, Bruce, and Armstrong, Beverly. *Puppets From Polyfoam: Spong-ees*. Walnut Creek CA: Early Stages, 1975.
Currel, David. *The Complete Book of Puppetry*. Boston: Plays, 1975.
Hunt, Tamara, and Renfro, Nancy. *Puppetry in Early Childhood Education*. Nancy Renfro Studios, 1982.
Luckin, Joyce. *Easy to Make Puppets*. Boston: Plays, 1975.
McLaren, Esmé. *Making Glove Puppets*. Boston: Plays, 1973.
Renfro, Nancy. *Puppetry and the Art of Story Creation*. Nancy Renfro Studios, 1979.
————. *Making Amazing Puppets*. Nancy Renfro Studios/Learning Works, 1980.
Ross, Laura. *Puppet Shows Using Poems and Stories*. New York: Lothrop, Lee and Shepard, 1970.

Biographies

Blair, Gwenda. *Laura Ingalls Wilder*. Illustrated by Thomas B. Allen. New York: Putnam, 1981.

Edwards, Anne. *The Great Houdini.* Illustrated by Joseph Ciardiello. New York: Putnam, 1977.

Fritz, Jean. *And Then What Happened, Paul Revere?* Illustrated by Margot Tomes. New York: Scholastic, 1973.

Johnson, Spencer. *The Value of Curiosity—the Story of Christopher Columbus.* San Diego CA: Value Communications, 1977.

McGovern, Anne. *If You Grew Up with Abraham Lincoln.* Illustrated by Brinton Turkle. New York: Scholastic, 1966.

Index

Index